Samuel French Acting Edition

The Keen Collection
One Acts by Contemporary Playwrights
Volume 6

Winifred and Myrtle
Go to High School
by Leah Nanako Winkler

Around 2
by James Anthony Tyler

The Caribbean Queen
Music by Salomon Lerner
Book and Lyrics by
Jamie Cowperthwait

SAMUELFRENCH.COM   SAMUELFRENCH.CO.UK

Winifred and Myrtle Go to High School Copyright © 2019
by Leah Nanako Winkler
Around 2 Copyright © 2019 by James Anthony Tyler
The Caribbean Queen Copyright © 2019 by Salomon Lerner
and Jamie Cowperthwait
All Rights Reserved

THE KEEN COLLECTION: VOLUME 6 is fully protected under the copyright laws of the United States of America, the British Commonwealth, including Canada, and all other countries of the Copyright Union. All rights, including professional and amateur stage productions, recitation, lecturing, public reading, motion picture, radio broadcasting, television and the rights of translation into foreign languages are strictly reserved.

ISBN 978-0-573-70779-7

www.SamuelFrench.com
www.SamuelFrench.co.uk

FOR PRODUCTION ENQUIRIES

UNITED STATES AND CANADA
Info@SamuelFrench.com
1-866-598-8449

UNITED KINGDOM AND EUROPE
Plays@SamuelFrench.co.uk
020-7255-4302

Each title is subject to availability from Samuel French, depending upon country of performance. Please be aware that *THE KEEN COLLECTION: VOLUME 6* may not be licensed by Samuel French in your territory. Professional and amateur producers should contact the nearest Samuel French office or licensing partner to verify availability.

CAUTION: Professional and amateur producers are hereby warned that *THE KEEN COLLECTION: VOLUME 6* is subject to a licensing fee. Publication of this play(s) does not imply availability for performance. Both amateurs and professionals considering a production are strongly advised to apply to Samuel French before starting rehearsals, advertising, or booking a theatre. A licensing fee must be paid whether the title(s) is presented for charity or gain and whether or not admission is charged. Professional/Stock licensing fees are quoted upon application to Samuel French.

No one shall make any changes in this title(s) for the purpose of production. No part of this book may be reproduced, stored in a retrieval system, or transmitted in any form, by any means, now known or yet to be invented, including mechanical, electronic, photocopying, recording, videotaping, or otherwise, without the prior written permission of the publisher. No one shall upload this title(s), or part of this title(s), to any social media websites.

For all enquiries regarding motion picture, television, and other media rights, please contact Samuel French.

MUSIC USE NOTE

Licensees are solely responsible for obtaining formal written permission from copyright owners to use copyrighted music in the performance of this play and are strongly cautioned to do so. If no such permission is obtained by the licensee, then the licensee must use only original music that the licensee owns and controls. Licensees are solely responsible and liable for all music clearances and shall indemnify the copyright owners of the play(s) and their licensing agent, Samuel French, against any costs, expenses, losses and liabilities arising from the use of music by licensees. Please contact the appropriate music licensing authority in your territory for the rights to any incidental music.

IMPORTANT BILLING AND CREDIT REQUIREMENTS

If you have obtained performance rights to this title, please refer to your licensing agreement for important billing and credit requirements.

TABLE OF CONTENTS

About Keen Teens 7

Keen Teens Angels...9

Winifred and Myrtle Go to High School 11

Around 2... 41

The Caribbean Queen 69

ABOUT KEEN TEENS

Founded in 2000, Keen Company is an award-winning Off-Broadway theater producing stories about the decisive moments that change us. The cornerstone of the company's outreach and educational efforts is Keen Teens. The program improves the quality of plays written for high school students by commissioning scripts from accomplished New York City playwrights. This free program for students provides invaluable mentorship opportunities – working alongside professional writers, directors, and designers to rehearse and premiere new work.

When first creating Keen Teens in 2007, the company found that teachers did not have access to material that was intended for a high school stage. Educators were left with either presenting classic plays never designed for teen actors, or producing simple skits that lacked rich material relevant to modern students. Central to Keen Company's mission is to produce theatre that patrons can identify with and connect to, however no such material existed for students and educators. Keen Teens brings the company's values to the high school stage by developing new work tailored specifically to be relevant and engaging to teen actors and audiences.

Keen Teens commissions and presents work that speaks to teens on their level, creating work that is as complex and multilayered as the high school world. Form, style, and context vary amongst each playwright and season. Topics have included cyberbullying and teen suicide (*Why Aren't You Dead Already?* by Halley Feiffer), same-sex relationships amongst athletes (*Going Left* by Kristoffer Diaz), environmental concerns (*A Polar Bear in New Jersey* by Anna Moench), death within a family (*Syd Arthur* by Kenny Finkle), and even the perils of YouTube fame (*30 Million* by Max Vernon and Jason Kim). All pieces deal honestly and provocatively with their subject matter – some through comedy and farce, some through sincerity and intimate portraits.

As well as being tailored to the social and emotional world of teens, each piece is also designed to be accessible to educators and drama festivals. Commissions consist of thirty-minute plays, simple designs, large casts, and flexible genders. These requirements are designed so that high schools might include as many students as possible and present their productions on their own, in an evening, or as part of a competition.

Every year the Keen Teens program culminates in the world premiere performances of three newly commissioned one-act plays at the Lion Theatre in Theater Row, New York City. Since 2005,

Keen Teens has made possible the Off-Broadway debut of over three hundred young actors and has led to the publication of over twenty-five new one-act plays. These plays are regularly produced not only in the United States, but in various countries around the world, from Australia to Singapore.

For more information, please visit www.keencompany.org/teens.

Keen Teens Staff

Robert Ross Parker, *Keen Teens Artistic Producer*
Hope Chavez, *Keen Teens Managing Producer*
Jeremy Stoller, *Director of New Work*

Keen Company

Jonathan Silverstein, *Artistic Director*
Ashley DiGiorgi, *Managing Producer*

KEEN TEENS ANGELS

Keen Teens is generously supported by the Axe-Houghton Foundation, as well as a group of donors affectionately called the Keen Teens Angels.

Emily Ackerman, Kassandra Adams and Nathanial Vaught, Lindsay Adkins, Linda Azarian, Grace Beggins, William and Casey Bradford, Karen Bradford, Sara Brandston, Paul Brill, Peter Bumcrot, Toby Butterfield, Nadja Caulfield, Kathleen Chalfant, Kathy Chazen and Larry Miller, Maria Cicio, Gary and Ellen Cohen, Katie Cohen, Elizabeth Corradino, Rose Courtney, Alexander Coxe, Michael Cristofer, Katharine Crost, Joanna D'Angelo, Michela Daliana, Nathanial Day, Mia Dillon, Marie DiSalvo, Linda D'Onofrio, Maralène Downs, Tony Fingleton, Kenny Finkle, Patricia Follert, Cathy Frankel, Mike Fresco, Sharon Friedland, Jack Gilpin and Anne McDonough, Douglas Giombarrese, Beth Gittleman, Wendy Goldstein, Greg Graham, Tim Grandia, Roberta Greenberg and Robert Goldy, Jose Gutierrez, Barbara McIntyre Hack, Dave Hall, Richard and Edith Hanley, Sarah Hauser, Daoud Heidami, Stuart Himmelfarb, Victoria Leacock Hoffman, Kimberly Howard, Robyn Huffman, Frank Iryami, David and Kate Kies, Madeline and Walter Marzano-Lesnevich, Marsha Mason, Eugenia McGill, David McMahon, Trevor Middleton, Nancy Morgan, Jasmine Nielsen, Marianna Noto, Matt O'Grady, Michael Ostroff, Paresh Patel, David and Faith Pedowitz, David Piening, Dave and Katherine Rabinowitz, John Rothman, David Schmidt, Matt Servitto, Susan Shapiro and Bob Piller, Charles Snipe and Robert Furlong, Olga Staffen, Patricia Stockhausen and Michael Emmerman, Jason Tam, Therese Tolomeo, Cathryn and Curtis Williamson, Alban Wilson, Michael Wolk, Allen and Marie Wolpert, Ernest and Judith Wong, Alan Zucker, Anonymous.

WINIFRED AND MYRTLE GO TO HIGH SCHOOL

Leah Nanako Winkler

WINIFRED AND MYRTLE GO TO HIGH SCHOOL was first produced by Keen Company at Theatre Row in New York City from May 11-13, 2018. The performance was directed by Michael Goldfried, with assistant direction by Patrick Dooley, scenic design by An-Lin Dauber, costume design by Karen Boyer, lighting design by Kate August, and sound design by Käri Berntson. The production stage manager was Marisa Ayerst. The cast was as follows:

WINIFRED . . . . Holliday Senquiz
MYRTLE . . . . Josi Oz
YOUNG WINIFRED . . . . A'dreana Williams
YOUNG MYRTLE . . . . Emerson Thomas-Gregory
EUGENE THE DOG . . . . Ashley Rivas
MR. WITHERS . . . . Rayna Brown
ALYSSA . . . . Eden Ann Anderson
BRANDON . . . . Julio Velazquez
CHEERLEADER 1 . . . . Amberrain E. Andrews
CHEERLEADER 2 . . . . Lanika Lee
GARY . . . . Jacob Bergman
GOTH KID . . . . Josi Oz
JOCK . . . . Angel Encarnacion
NERD . . . . Brea White

CHARACTERS

WINIFRED – 100 years old. Spunky, outgoing. Can be a little hot-headed but is kind and sensitive inside. She was a bit wild in her heyday but Myrtle, her very best friend, always grounds her.

MYRTLE – 100 years old. A little shy. Thoughtful. Can be a little nervous sometimes, but Winifred, her very best friend, always calms her down.

YOUNG WINIFRED – 100 years old in a 15-year-old girl's body. A total babe and knows it.

YOUNG MYRTLE – 100 years old in a 15-year-old girl's body. A total babe but doesn't know it. She wears glasses.

EUGENE THE DOG – A very very very very very very very very very very very very very very very very very very old dog. Kind, faithful. But again, very very very old.

MR. WITHERS – A 120-year-old school teacher.

ALYSSA – 15, the head cheerleader. More than meets the eye.

CHEERLEADERS 1, 2, 3 – Alyssa's crew. They're pretty and smart but can have sassy mean streaks.

GOTH GIRL – A goth. Can be amended to Goth Person. Has a lot of feelings boiling underneath the surface.

BRANDON – 15, a mean jock who has a bright future.

GARY – 15, a cute tech geek with a vast knowledge of DJ equipment. Loves movies where people time-travel or switch bodies like *Freaky Friday* and *The Hot Chick*.

ENSEMBLE – A group of teens who can portray members of various cliques. They also double as vacationers.

All roles can be played by any ethnicity. Please have as much diversity as possible. Gender is also flexible and fluid.

Scene One
Something Magical Happens to Winifred and Myrtle!

> (**WINIFRED** and **MYRTLE** sit across from each other at a table. Their dog, **EUGENE**, lays nearby. Everyone is very, very, very old.)
>
> (There is a birthday cake on the table with a big candle in it. The candle is in the shape of the number 100. **WINIFRED** and **MYRTLE** stare at each other for a bit. And then:)

WINIFRED. (It is difficult for her to sing, but she does.)
HAPPY BIRTHDAY TO YOU.
HAPPY BIRTHDAY TO YOU.
HAPPY BIRTHDAY DEAR MYRTLE.
HAPPY BIRTHDAY TO YOU.

EUGENE. (It is difficult for him to bark.) Wooooooooooooo huuuuf. *[To you!!]*

WINIFRED. Your turn.

MYRTLE. Aw Winifred, you bearcat! You know I get shy when I sing!

WINIFRED. You're always a little shy, Myrtle! That's just who you are. But you've always had such a wonderful voice. Ever since we were in grade school.

MYRTLE. That was so long ago.

EUGENE. Wooohoooof. *[Yep.]*

WINIFRED. You may be old now, pal but you're still the same gal! My number one buddy – my partner in crime!

EUGENE. Woohoof. *[What about me?]*

WINIFRED. You too, Eugene. You too. The three of us. Best friends forever.

EUGENE. Woof! *[That's more like it!]*

MYRTLE. *(This gets to **MYRTLE**.)* Alright. Alright, here goes nothing. But only because you brought up the best friend thing. You *know* I've gotten sentimental with age!

WINIFRED. *(To **EUGENE**.)* She was *always* sentimental.

EUGENE. Woof Woof. *[True.]*

MYRTLE.
>HAPPY BIRTHDAY TO YOU TOO.
>HAPPY BIRTHDAY TO YOU TOO.
>HAPPY BIRTHDAY DEAR MYRTLE...TOO.
>HAPPY BIRTHDAY TO YOU TOO!

>*(**WINIFRED** claps. **MYRTLE** really is a wonderful singer.)*

WINIFRED. That's the berries. Now let's blow out our candles and cut the cake.

>*(**WINIFRED** and **MYRTLE** blow out their birthday candles. It is very difficult for the both of them. **MYRTLE** cuts the cake into three pieces. She gives one pieces to **WINIFRED** and one piece to herself. Then she gives one giant piece to **EUGENE**. **EUGENE** eats with great energy. This should be a visual gag.)*

That dog can eat. Doesn't matter how old he gets.

MYRTLE. It's so weird how we've outlived all of our friends.

WINIFRED. And our friends' pets.

MYRTLE. Maybe it's just the power of our strong female friendship.

WINIFRED. That's a nice thought, Myrtle. A nice thought indeed.

>*(**MYRTLE** and **WINIFRED** also eat.)*

MYRTLE. Did you have a good day Winifred? Anything new while I was taking my nap?

WINIFRED. Not really. The boredom set in. I want to be out in the world Myrtle. But my bones won't let me down those damned stairs!

(**EUGENE** *doesn't look good.*)

(*He dry-heaves.*)

MYRTLE. Look what you've done now Winifred! Your cursing made Eugene upset!

WINIFRED. Bushwa!

(**MYRTLE** *gasps.*)

MYRTLE. Such a potty mouth! What has gotten into you?

WINIFRED. Oh. Absolutely nothing. For a very long time. And that's *exactly* the problem! What's even the point anymore Myrtle? I feel like we ain't livin'!

MYRTLE. Don't you dare Winifred! We're VERY lucky to be alive. My husband and your three husbands went to the great speakeasy in the sky loooong ago!

WINIFRED. Yeah! And they're probably drinkin' gin and dancin' the Charleston! Which is more than what we're doing Myrtle! Apple sauce! Bein' old is hard. And there's more to life than just being alive. Don't you remember Myrtle? Don't you remember when we were just a coupl'a girls?

MYRTLE. I sure do, Winifred. I sure do.

WINIFRED. We would booze! Dance! Go to the beach! Oh – and how we'd smoke cigars and go all the way! Those were some wacky days. Weren't they?

MYRTLE. I dunno Winifred. I've always felt like a cancelled stamp.

WINIFRED. Didn't I bring you out of your shell?

MYRTLE. That you did. Hey. Do you remember that cinder dick? The one who was just about as cute as a bug's ear –

WINIFRED. Oh yes! He filled me with such daylight. What I wouldn't give to have a fella like that once again.

MYRTLE. What about your husbands Winifred!

WINIFRED. Who cares! Give me that cinder dick!

MYRTLE. You tart!

(*They laugh.*)

WINIFRED. We really did know where the real hootenanny was back then, didn't we?

MYRTLE. We sure did, pal.

EUGENE. Wooof. *[More cake.]*

MYRTLE. Winifred. You were such a hotsy totsy.

EUGENE. Wooof. *[More cake.]*

WINIFRED. And you were a piece of calico Myrtle! Oh, how I wish we were young again.

MYRTLE. How young? Forty? Seventy?

WINIFRED. Fifteen. Cuz that was the beginning of everything.

MYRTLE. So much to look forward to. So much to learn. I wish we were fifteen again too!

EUGENE. WOOOF!! *[More cake!!]*

> *(A magical sound cue.* All of a sudden the lights flicker! Then they go back to normal. A beat.* **MYRTLE** *and* **WINIFRED** *shrug.)*

WINIFRED. What the heck was that?

MYRTLE. Eugene's whining darned near blew the fuse out. Go to bed Eugene! You're too hyper! No more cake for you!

EUGENE. Woof. *[Fine, okay, cry cry cry.]*

MYRTLE. You know, for a second I thought maybe our birthday wish was coming true. Like in those movies where people switch bodies or become Rob Schneider.

WINIFRED. Well if I've learned anything in my one hundred years of living as a woman on Planet Earth – it's that birthday wishes don't always come true, Myrtle.

MYRTLE. I guess they don't Winifred. I guess they don't.

WINIFRED. Alright doll face. It's getting late! Six p.m. is waaaaaay past my bedtime. Isn't that right Eugene?

---

*A license to produce *Winifred and Myrtle Go to High School* does not include a performance license for any third-party or copyrighted music. Licensees should create an original composition or use music in the public domain. For further information, please see Music Use Note on page 3.

(Pause.)

Eugene?

ARE YOU ALIVE?

*(**EUGENE** snores into his cake.)*

MYRTLE. He's just having a beautiful dream.
WINIFRED. See you in the morning love.
MYRTLE. See you in the morning.

*(**WINIFRED** and **MYRTLE** exit, leaving **EUGENE** asleep on the floor – having a beautiful dream. Then a slow burning light becomes so bright that we think we might be in the sun. Music.* A crescendo. Blackout. The sound of a rooster and we transition into...)*

---

*A license to produce *Winifred and Myrtle Go to High School* does not include a performance license for any third-party or copyrighted music. Licensees should create an original composition or use music in the public domain. For further information, please see Music Use Note on page 3.

Scene Two
Winifred and Myrtle are Fifteen Again!

(Next morning. **YOUNG MYRTLE** *enters. She is fifteen years old but is still walking like an old person and wearing the same outfit from the night before, yawning.)*

YOUNG MYRTLE. Another day. Another morning. What time is it? Oh! Already five a.m.? So late for me. But murder! I feel SO awake today. So much energy! I seem to have an extra skip in my step! Why. Why I feel like I can run! Can I run? No Myrtle. Of course, you can't. Of course...

(She runs.)

OH MY GOODNESS OH MY GOODNESS I'M RUNNING I'M RUNNING I'M RUNNING! WOW I HAVEN'T RUN IN YEARS! MAYBE DECADES! No pain in my usual spots. Oh! And I can stand up straight!! WINIFRED, EUGENE GET IN HERE! I'M STANDING UP STRAIGHT!

*(***EUGENE*** enters. He is still old. Then he starts growling. Well...***EUGENE***'s version of growling.)*

EUGENE. GRRRROOOOFFFFHHH!!! *[Ahhh who are you?!]*

YOUNG MYRTLE. Eugene, why on earth are you growling? You've done lost your mind. Come here boy-o! It's just me. Myrtle.

EUGENE. BARK. BARK. BARK. BARK! *[Prove it!]*

YOUNG MYRTLE. Prove it? Fine. Remember boy-o? I found you in the rain when you were just a pup. I let you in the house even though Ma and Pop said they'd kill me if I tried. There wasn't much food on the table during the Depression not even for humans. That's right. The Great Depression. We go waaay back, pal. Now, let's do our special handshake that only the two of us know.

EUGENE. Barrrrk. *[Okay, I'll try it.]*

(**EUGENE** *and* **YOUNG MYRTLE** *do the handshake. It's delightful.* **EUGENE** *jumps on* **YOUNG MYRTLE** *and licks her.*)

EUGENE. Bark bark bark! *[It's you! It's really you! Oh my gosh you look amazing!]*

YOUNG MYRTLE. Oh, Eugene you're acting so weird. I haven't changed my appearance at all. I think you must be ill. Let me feel your head.

(**YOUNG MYRTLE** *leans down and feels* **EUGENE***'s head.*)

YOUNG MYRTLE. You don't *feel* warm.

(*A realization.*) Wait a minute! Bending down didn't take seventeen minutes like it usually does. And here I am, able to pop right back up to a standing position! What on dear earth is going on with me?

(*All of a sudden we hear a scream.*)

EUGENE. BARK BARK BARK! *[What the heck?]*

YOUNG MYRTLE. Winifred?? Why are you screaming?

(**YOUNG WINIFRED** *enters, holding a handheld mirror.*)

AHHH WHO ARE YOU IMPOSTER!

YOUNG WINIFRED. MYRTLE!! ITS ME, WINIFRED!

YOUNG MYRTLE. BY GOLLY. IT *IS* YOU! EXCEPT YOU'RE...

YOUNG WINIFRED. FIFTEEN! AND MYRTLE, LOOK!

EUGENE. BARK BARK BARK!

YOUNG WINFRED. YOU'RE FIFTEEN TOO!

(**YOUNG WINIFRED** *shows* **YOUNG MYRTLE** *her reflection in the handheld mirror.*)

YOUNG MYRTLE. (*Seeing her reflection.*) HOT SPIT AND MONKEY VOMIT!

YOUNG WINIFRED. Our birthday wish came true!

(**EUGENE** *faints dramatically.*)

(*Blackout.*)

Scene Three
Winifred and Myrtle Go to High School!

*(Later that day on a high school campus. A diverse group of high school **STUDENTS** enter. They are mingling with the typical high school cliques. Most of them hold smartphones. Some are taking selfies, snaps, etc. Some are talking, etc.)*

*(A lone **GOTH GIRL** reads a book of Emily Dickinson poems, alone. **BRANDON**, a jock, passes around a ball with his teammates. **ALYSON**, a cheerleader, commiserates with **CHEERLEADERS 1, 2,** and **3**. They practice a cheer routine. It's good and athletic.)*

*(**YOUNG MYRTLE** and **YOUNG WINIFRED** enter – wearing the same clothes from Scenes One and Two. They look completely out of place, mainly because of their old-people clothes. A few **STUDENTS** pause to look at them. Maybe some laugh. Maybe some are intrigued.)*

YOUNG WINIFRED. *(Frustrated.)* Mildred, I still don't understand why you wanted to come to high school when we could've been at the gin mill by now!

YOUNG MYRTLE. *(Moony.)* Just five minutes, Winifred. Why, this is our old stompin' grounds for goodness' sakes! Don't you just feel so...dreamy?

YOUNG WINIFRED. Honestly, I just feel thirsty.

YOUNG MYRTLE. And oh my! Look over there!

*(Pointing to **GOTH GIRL**.)*

See that little girl reading by herself in the corner?

YOUNG WINIFRED. Little girl? More like Wednesday Addams!

YOUNG MYRTLE. That's the very corner where I used to sit before class. And she's reading the same book I used to read! Emily Dickinson!

(To **GOTH GIRL**.*)* Hello there!

(Reciting from memory.) I'm Nobody! Who are you?

Are you – Nobody – too?

Then there's a pair of us!

Don't tell! They'd advertise – you know!

GOTH GIRL. WHY CAN'T PEOPLE JUST LEAVE ME ALONE?! I'M GOING THROUGH SOMETHING SIGNIFICANT IN MY HEART!

YOUNG WINIFRED. And I'm going through something significant in my loins! Come on Myrtle, your five minutes is up! Let's go meet some fellas at the gin mill!

YOUNG MYRTLE. I keep telling you Winifred – they *don't make* gin mills anymore. The Prohibition is over!

> *(***YOUNG WINIFRED** *pulls out a bottle of gin to celebrate.)*

YOUNG WINIFRED. And thank all high power for that!

YOUNG MYRTLE. Put that away you inappropriate bim! This is a place of learning!

> *(***YOUNG MYRTLE** *tries to take the gin from* **YOUNG WINIFRED**. *There is a funny struggle. However, this works –* **ALYSSA** *takes note and approaches* **YOUNG MYRTLE** *and* **YOUNG WINIFRED** *with* **CHEERLEADERS 1, 2,** *and* **3**.*)*

ALYSSA. Well hello ladies. You must be new in school.

YOUNG WINIFRED. Oh kid, we've been waaaay around the block you don't even know.

YOUNG MYRTLE. Actually – what my pal here meant to say was *(Trying to sound young.)* sure. Whatever. Like. Coolness and beans. Groovy. Aesthetic? Fluuu Fluu...

YOUNG WINIFRED. FLEEK. IT'S FLEEK. MYRTLE. IT'S FLEEK.

ALYSSA. Um. I'm just gonna pretend like that didn't happen.

CHEERLEADER 1. Yeah, the word fleek is really overused in pop culture when adults try to write teens and it's really annoying because it's actually not a thing.

CHEERLEADER 2. Neither is going super viral super easily. Like. It's actually really hard to go viral.

CHEERLEADER 1. Like it's an accomplishment.

ALYSSA. Anyways. Where'd you get that booze?

YOUNG WINIFRED. Straight outta my cabinet.

ALYSSA. Wow. Stealing from your parents. How...bold. What's your name?

YOUNG WINIFRED. I'm Winifred and this is my best pal Myrtle.

CHEERLEADER 3. Are those like – your real names?

CHEERLEADER 2. Or your snap names?

YOUNG WINIFRED. What the heck is a snap name?

ALYSSA. You know – like Snapchat?

YOUNG WINIFRED. Snapchat eh? Is that when you snap while you're chattin' up someone? *(Snapping.)* Like this? Hello! Hello! I'm chatting! And now I want to sinnnng!

(Snapping.) Hello, my baby, hello my honey,
Hello my ragtime, summertime gal.

CHEERLEADER 1. What is happening right now.

YOUNG MYRTLE. Winifred and Myrtle are our real names!

CHEERLEADER 2. That's like so...

ALYSSA. *(Earnest.)* Retro!

CHEERLEADER 3. Yeah!

CHEERLEADERS 1, 2 & 3. Like, so retro!

(**YOUNG WINIFRED** *takes a swig of gin.*)

YOUNG WINIFRED. Wow getting ossified is so easy when your body is viral.

ALYSSA. Ossified?

YOUNG WINIFRED. Crooched! Splifficated! Zozzled! It's nine a.m. and I'm goin' on a toot! WOOOOT!

ALYSSA. You're fun. Can we have some?

YOUNG WINIFRED. Sure!

YOUNG MYRTLE. WINIFRED. ARE YOU TRYING TO GET US ARRESTED?!?! WE DO NOT SERVE ALCOHOL TO MINORS!

ALYSSA. But you're minors.

CHEERLEADER 1. Yeah. What's up your lame friend's butt?

YOUNG WINIFRED. *Hey! Myrtle is not lame! I can't believe I almost gave you my giggle juice! You...You...YOU WET BLANKETS!*

(**CHEERLEADERS 1, 2,** *and* **3** *gasp.*)

ALYSSA. *(Getting in* **YOUNG WINIFRED***'s face.)* What did you say to me?

YOUNG WINIFRED. *(Getting in her face back.) I said you're a wet blanket.*

ALYSSA. *(Still in her face.)* Is that bad?

YOUNG WINIFRED. *It's very very bad.*

(**CHEERLEADERS 1, 2,** *and* **3** *gasp again.*)

CHEERLEADER 1. Who do you think you're talking to *new girl*? *This is OUR school.*

YOUNG WINIFRED. I think I'm talking to a little girl. A little girl who's too big for her own britches.

ALYSSA. *I'm not wearing britches.*

YOUNG WINIFRED. Well maybe you should be. Because your skirt leaves little to the imagination!

RANDO STUDENT 1. No, she did not!

RANDO STUDENT 2. Ooooooooh. Fight!

(The rest of the **STUDENTS** *have started to gather around. More than a few of them have taken out their phones. The* **GOTH GIRL** *cries into her book.)*

GOTH GIRL. *(Crying.)* DESPITE MY CHOICE OF DARK CLOTHING AND GOTHIC MAKEUP I JUST WANT WORLD PEACE!!

BRANDON. *You* got *got* Alyssa!

(*The* **STUDENTS** *whoop and holler.* **ALYSSA** *and* **YOUNG WINIFRED** *are in each other's faces. More* **STUDENTS** *take out their phones. Except* **GOTH GIRL**, *who is still crying.*)

YOUNG MYRTLE. That is grammatically incorrect sir! And everyone, please clam down.

GOTH GIRL. YES, PLEASE CALM DOWN PLEASE FOR THE SAKE OF THE FUTURE OF THIS COUNTRY!!

STUDENT 3. HEY YO!!

YOUNG WINIFRED. (*Looking around at the* **STUDENTS** *who are filming.*) Why is everyone pointing those little boxes at me?

GOTH GIRL. (*Crying.*) BECAUSE EVERYONE IS OBSESSED WITH TECHNOLOGY AND WE CAN'T LIVE IN THE MOMENT. I JUST WANT TO LIVE IN A LIBRARY!

YOUNG MYRTLE. They're phones Winifred! Just like the ones we see in the commercials. This isn't sitting right with me, pal. Thanks for sticking up for me – but I think it's time for us to go.

(*Overly paranoid.*) I don't wanna be recorded and have the government steal all our assets!

BRANDON. Hey – that chick sounds just like my grandma! WHAT UP GRANNIE. YOU GOT GRANNIE PANTS UNDER DEM PJS?

(*The* **STUDENTS** *laugh.*)

YOUNG WINIFRED. DO NOT TALK ABOUT MYRTLE'S UNDERWEAR! ALSO, SHE'S NOT A GRANDMA. SHE IS RETRO!!

YOUNG MYRTLE. Well, technically I am a grandma. But. Okay.

ALYSSA. AND YOU'RE NOT RETRO. I TAKE THAT BACK.

CHEERLEADERS 1, 2 & 3. YEAH, WE TAKE IT BACK!

YOUNG WINIFRED. APPLE SAUCE!!

STUDENTS. *(Chanting.)* FIGHT FIGHT FIGHT FIGHT FIGHT FIGHT!

ALYSSA & YOUNG WINIFRED. *(Going in for the attack.)* AHHHHHHHH!!

> *(***YOUNG MYRTLE*** holds ***YOUNG WINIFRED*** back. The ***STUDENTS*** lose it.)*

GOTH GIRL. I'M OVERWHELMED!!

> *(Everyone stops and looks at ***GOTH GIRL***.)*

How dreary – to be – Somebody!

How public – like a Frog –

To tell one's name – the livelong June –

To an admiring Bog!

I HOPE EMILY DICKINSON IS IN HEAVEN RIDING UNICORNS AND EATING COTTON CANDY GOODBYEEEEE!

> *(***GOTH GIRL*** runs away, legs flailing.)*

BRANDON. That was weird.

ALYSSA. And this isn't over. Freak.

> *(The ***CHEERLEADERS*** gasp. The students go "ooooooooh.")*

You. Me. Cafeteria. Lunch.

YOUNG WINIFRED. *...What about lunch? I usually have breakfast, supper, and a good night's sleep.*

ALYSSA. UGH. JUST BE THERE YOU WEIRDO. Ladies – let's go!

(To **YOUNG WINIFRED** *and* **YOUNG MYRTLE***.)* Nice outfits by the way.

YOUNG WINIFRED. Thanks!

ALYSON. THAT WAS A LIE. I WAS LYING. HAHAHA HAHAHA!

> *(The ***CHEERLEADERS*** laugh and exit. Some more whooping and hollering. The second bell rings. The ***STUDENTS*** start to file out.*

MR. WITHERS, *a very, very, very old teacher, enters.)*

MR. WITHERS. Come on now. Hurry up students. Being late can ruin opportunities and shape your reputation in the future!

(**BRANDON** *does something stupid.*)

OH BRANDON! ENOUGH. YOU'RE NOT AS FUNNY AS YOU THINK YOU ARE YOUNG MAN – AND THE SOONER YOU LEARN THE BETTER.

(**BRANDON** *makes a fart noise with his lips. Only a few people laugh.*)

RANDO STUDENT 3. *(To* **BRANDON***.)* Mr. Withers is right. It's exhausting to fake laugh at your jokes. I don't know why I still do it. My crush on you has faded.

(*Everyone except for* **YOUNG MYRTLE**, **YOUNG WINIFRED**, *and* **MR. WITHERS** *exits.*)

YOUNG MYRTLE. Mr. Withers?? Gee wilickers, did that young lady just say Mr. Withers??

MR. WITHERS. That's my name.

YOUNG MYRTLE. Jiminy Crickets! It's me! Myrtle! Your favorite student from way back when!
I can't believe you still teach here. What are you? Two hundred years old?

MR. WITHERS. And for that – you're going straight to detention! And let the record hold! I'm only one hundred and twenty!!

(*Pause.*)

I don't know why I've lived this long. I like to think it's because I like to help people. And oh, how I love teaching. I fundamentally believe in the pursuit of professional competence. You're always learning just as much as you're teaching. Always aware of the impact you have on society. When you do something that you love, then you live, girls. Oh, how you live. Your life becomes *beautiful*.

YOUNG WINIFRED. Wow Mr. Withers I really thought you'd be tired by now.

MR. WITHERS. I may be tired but I am filled with motivation. To SEND YOU TWO TO DETENTION!

> (**MR. WITHERS** *hands* **YOUNG WINIFRED** *and* **YOUNG MYRTLE** *detention slips and exits.*)

YOUNG MYRTLE. I don't think Mr. Withers recognized us.

YOUNG WINIFRED. Yeah there's like no way he knows we're two old biddies who wished we were fifteen again and woke up in our teen-aged bodies.

GARY. Two old biddies in fifteen-year-old bodies eh?

> (**YOUNG WINIFRED** *and* **YOUNG MYRTLE** *scream.*)

YOUNG WINIFRED. AHHH you scared us. Our hearts!! I'm having a heart attack!

YOUNG MYRTLE. No, you aren't Winifred. Remember?? We're young?

YOUNG WINIFRED. Oh. Right. What do you want kid? Now that you've overheard our secret!

GARY. Nothing! I just think it's cool. I love movies where people shapeshift, go back in time or switch bodies. It fills me with glee and inspires me to look deeply at my life and how I can change my ways. Do you know the logistics of your granted wish? Like, the perimeters and the rules behind it?

YOUNG WINIFRED. Actually...we have no idea.

GARY. Well. You should figure it out. Before it's too late. DON DON DOOOOM.

> (**GARY** *exits mysteriously.* **YOUNG MYRTLE** *and* **YOUNG WINIFRED** *are left alone.*)

YOUNG MYRTLE. Too late? What does he mean "too late"?

YOUNG WINIFRED. Maybe he's talking about our wish expiring. Maybe we're only young for a limited amount of time!

YOUNG WINIFRED. Poo! There's no way I'd wanna be old again.

YOUNG MYRTLE. Maybe being old doesn't have to be so bad? I mean – *Mr. Withers* is full of life.
Maybe being around what you love is the key to staying alive.

YOUNG WINIFRED. I don't know Myrtle. Many who are loved lose their lives randomly and cruelly.
I think it's luck. And a little bit of magic. And a whole lot of jungle juice. ANYWAY, I'm tired of thinkin'! This is too much philosophy for the morning! We got work to do.

YOUNG MYRTLE. What kinda work?

YOUNG WINIFRED. Teaching those cheerleaders a lesson! Come on. Let's blouse!

YOUNG MYRTLE. But Winifred – what about detention?

YOUNG WINIFRED. Detention?! I'm not going to no DETENTION! I'm Winifred Hannigan, I'm a hundred years old and I can do whatever the hell I want!

YOUNG MYRTLE. I don't know Winifred. I forgot how scary high school can be. And I miss our Eugene. Maybe we should go home.

(**EUGENE** *enters.*)

EUGENE. Bark bark bark! *[I'm right here! I'm right here!]*

YOUNG MYRTLE. Eugene! You're here!

YOUNG WINIFRED. See! We're all together. And you know what that means Myrtle? It means we're already home. Now help me get some cash out of my fanny pack.

(**YOUNG MYRTLE** *digs out a fanny pack from inside* **YOUNG WINIFRED**'s *long nightgown.* **EUGENE** *tries to help. It is a struggle. But when they finally get to it – there is a bunch of cash. Some great physical humor here between* **YOUNG WINIFRED**, **YOUNG MYRTLE**, *and* **EUGENE**, *who eventually saves the day. Then –* **EUGENE** *throws the money in the air like in a music video.*)

We're going shopping! Hey YO!!

YOUNG MYRTLE. HEY YO!!!!
EUGENE. Arf arf arffffff! *[Hey yooooo!]*
    (Blackout.)

Scene Four
Lunchtime!

*(School cafeteria. The **CHEERLEADERS**, **JOCKS**, **NERDS**, **DRAMA GEEKS**, etc. are sitting at their own tables. **BRANDON** approaches **ALYSSA**.)*

BRANDON. YO Alyssa, when is this fight gonna happen? It's gonna be dope af!

YOUNG MYRTLE. There isn't going to be a fight young man!

*(Everyone turns to see **YOUNG MYRTLE** and **YOUNG WINIFRED** decked out in full flapper gear.)*

RANDO STUDENT 4. Wow they look hot!

RANDO STUDENT 5. Hey miss – you got a date to prom?

GOTH GIRL. I'M SO CONFUSED RIGHT NOW.

YOUNG WINIFRED. Myrtle, Eugene and I commiserated and we don't believe in Woman on Woman Violence!

YOUNG MYRTLE. Yeah! We went through First AND Second-wave feminism!

YOUNG WINIFRED. Hit it Gary!

GARY. Got it Winifred!

(To audience.) Not only am I an expert in genre movies, I'm also an expert in DJ equipment!

*(**GARY** plays "Hello My Baby.")*

YOUNG MYRTLE. This is a dance off!

BRANDON. A dance off!

NERD 1. A dance off??

DRAMA GEEK. DID SHE SAY DANCE OFF?!

JOCK 2. Stop being so dramatic drama geek.

DRAMA GEEK. I CAN'T HELP IT. DANCE OFFS ARE UH-MAZING!! AND LOOK AT THEIR OUTFITS! I'M FREAKING OUT! I'M FREAKING OUT! I'M FREAKING OUT! LOOK AT THEM GO! I'M GONNA DIE!!

(DRAMA GEEK pretends to die. A dance off begins. **YOUNG WINIFRED** *and* **YOUNG MYRTLE***'s amazing moves from the 1920s vs. the* **CHEERLEADERS***' cartwheels and modern-day dancing.* **EUGENE** *eventually enters, joining in on* **YOUNG WINIFRED** *and* **YOUNG MYRTLE***'s team. The crowd goes nuts for* **EUGENE***! This is* **EUGENE***'s big moment! Because of* **EUGENE***,* **YOUNG WINIFRED** *and* **YOUNG MYRTLE** *win the dance off! The crowd chants: "Go Winifred! Go Myrtle! Go Winifred. Go Myrtle. Go Eugene!! Eugene Eugene Eugene!!" Then* **BRANDON** *gets in* **ALYSSA***'s face with his phone.)*

BRANDON. Yo Alyssa. How does it feel to be a loser?

ALYSSA. Get that out of my face Brandon!

(Alyssa's voice replays on Brandon's phone and repeats, "Get that out of my face, Brandon!")

BRANDON. Fine – because I already put this on all of my social media platforms. So, BOOM. The whole internet will know you're a loser FOREVER. Because you know what Alyssa? THE INTERNET IS FOREVER!! HEY YO!!!!

YOUNG MYRTLE. Wow. That wasn't very nice.

ALYSSA. What do YOU care?

YOUNG MYRTLE. Me? I care *a lot*. About a lot of things, dear. And what that young man did was not right.

YOUNG WINIFRED. I agree!

ALYSSA. But my reputation is tarnished. My whole life is ruined!

*(***YOUNG WINIFRED** *and* **YOUNG MYRTLE** *burst into laughter.)*

YOUNG WINIFRED. Oh Alyssa. My dame! That's simply not true. It's not easy to go viral – remember?

YOUNG WINIFRED. And nobody was even really watching our little bonanza anyway. Everyone was looking at those brick-shaped thingies with their eyes glazed over.

CHEERLEADER 1. Brick-shaped thingies? Are you like – talking about our phones?

YOUNG WINIFRED. PHONES?! Children, stop your recording now! I told you – I don't want the government to – *(Looking at Cheerleader 1's phone.)* Hey, why do I look like a cute little kitten there?

CHEERLEADER 2. Uhh cuz it's a filter?

YOUNG WINIFRED. THAT'S THE BEST THING I'VE EVER SEEN! DO IT AGAIN.

> (**CHEERLEADER 2** *and* **YOUNG WINIFRED** *get distracted by Cheerleader 2's phone. They play with different filters.* **CHEERLEADERS 1** *and* **3** *go with them.*)

YOUNG MYRTLE. As I was saying, Alyssa dear. There's so much more to life than high school bullies who try to expose you on the computer screen! Why – my life didn't even begin until after high school.

ALYSSA. What do you mean? Aren't you in high school now?

YOUNG MYRTLE. YES! YES I AM! Uhhh I just mean – I KNOW that after high school, my real life will begin. It's a big world out there. So much will happen between fifteen and a hundred. You'll see.

ALYSSA. Wow Myrtle. You're like...so wise.

YOUNG MYRTLE. And you're the berries, Alyssa.

ALYSSA. Berries? I like that. I'm gonna start saying that.

YOUNG MYRTLE. You go ahead, dear.

ALYSSA. You're the berries, too. Myrtle. Just berries.

> (**ALYSSA** *and* **YOUNG MYRTLE** *hug.*)

YOUNG WINIFRED. Hey Myrtle! Myrtle! Get a load of these INSTANT GRAM stories! You can record the TV on the phone but the TV is you!! And you get all these bonus frames attached and watch yourself turn into animals or STEVE BUSCEMI! I used to think this generation was so shallow but really – they're just inventive! And capable of absorbing information on multiple levels! They're...what was the phrase again dear?

CHEERLEADER 2. Woke.

YOUNG WINIFRED. YES! WOKE! What a smart group of young people we have in this world. The future is bright!

YOUNG MYRTLE. That's just wonderful, Winifred! There really is more to these kids than everyone thinks.

ALYSSA. It's true. I feel misunderstood like all the time just because you know, I'm pretty or whatever.

When I grow up I want to be a doctor. Just because I'm a cheerleader – it doesn't mean I can't be smart. Women can be multiple things.

CHEERLEADER 1. I hate that phrase, "You can't have it all," because it's only like two things.

I want to be a doctor too but a veterinarian. I think animals are strong and wise. I love the earth.

JOCK 1. I want to be a father. Mine was never around. So, I want to be the best that I can be.

NERD 2. I'm going to be a politician. Sure, sometimes I get bullied – but that just gives me perspective to accept all. Also, I know bullies are just doing it out of pain.

BRANDON. And that's why I want to be a therapist. I'm in pain and therefore I lash out.

I hate doing it but I do. So, I'm going to work hard when I grow up to fix other people's pain.

I know how bad it hurts! I deleted the video, Alyssa. I'm really really sorry.

YOUNG WINIFRED. Wow. Everyone's so self-aware and smart.

DRAMA GEEK. I'M SO PROUD OF ALL OF US. GROUP HUG!!

> (*All of the* **STUDENTS** *group hug.* **YOUNG MYRTLE** *and* **YOUNG WINIFRED** *watch with delight.*)

YOUNG MYRTLE. Come on Winifred, I think our work here is done.

YOUNG WINIFRED. But Myrtle – we were having such a hoot.

YOUNG MYRTLE. You're right, Winifred. When you're right, you're right. But I realized something when I was talking to dear Alyssa. These kids – they have so much to live for – and we already lived it! I don't wanna do high school again Winifred. I'm too old for this!

YOUNG WINIFRED. So, what are you saying? That you wanna go home? Make another cake? Burn another candle? And wish all THIS away so that we can be old again because of your little epiphany? Because that would be way too –

YOUNG MYRTLE. Predictable?

YOUNG WINIFRED. Yeah!

YOUNG MYRTLE. I know! That's why I have a better idea! Go fetch Mr. Withers and meet me outside. I had Gary call us an Uber!

YOUNG WINIFRED. What's a goober?

GARY. Actually, I use Lyft. Uber doesn't agree with my political standpoints.

>   *(Pause.)*

Also, you might want to check up on your dog. He looks kinda...dead from the dance off.

>   (**EUGENE** *is in the corner, looking dead.*)

YOUNG WINIFRED. EUGENE!! BOOHOO!!!!

YOUNG MYRTLE. SAY IT AIN'T SO EUGENE SAY IT AIN'T SO!!

>   (**EUGENE** *finally jolts up.*)

EUGENE. Bark bark bark. *[I'm so tired.]*

YOUNG WINIFRED. Oh, thank goodness. He's just really tired.

EUGENE. Bark bark bark. *[I need a vacation.]*

YOUNG MYRTLE. A vacation? Well Eugene, you're in luck – because where we're about to go – tired doesn't even exist!

> *(YOUNG WINIFRED and YOUNG MYRTLE start to leave.)*

GARY. *(To YOUNG WINIFRED.)* Wait you're leaving?! Please no! I'm like in love with you!

YOUNG WINIFRED. You're just a boy!

BRANDON. But sophomores date seniors all the time!

YOUNG WINIFRED. I'M NOT THAT KIND OF SENIOR!

> *(YOUNG WINIFRED, YOUNG MYRTLE, and EUGENE go.)*

GARY. Waaaait!

> *(Whiteout. The sound of a plane taking off that slowly transforms into luau music.*)*

---

*A license to produce *Winifred and Myrtle Go to High School* does not include a performance license for any third-party or copyrighted music. Licensees should create an original composition or use music in the public domain. For further information, please see Music Use Note on page 3.

Scene Five
Winifred and Myrtle go to Maui!

(Lights up on Maui. Various **VACATIONERS** *have set up shop on the sand. Among them are* **YOUNG WINIFRED, YOUNG MYRTLE, EUGENE,** *and* **MR. WITHERS.***)*

MR. WITHERS. So let me get this straight! You just wished upon a birthday cake and THIS happened?

YOUNG MYRTLE. Yes sir. And we thought about going back to high school – doing the whole shebang.

YOUNG WINIFRED. But we decided just to take it easy.

YOUNG MYRTLE. Been there. Done that.

YOUNG WINIFRED. And if anyone needs a vacation Mr. Withers – it's you! So glad you could come with us.

YOUNG MYRTLE. So, so glad. Especially since we're technically too young to buy hooch! I'm running low Teach. Sneak us another?

MR. WITHERS. Bartender – I'm running a bit dry!

(The **BARTENDER** *approaches. Refills* **MR. WITHERS'** *extravagant cup. He shares it with* **YOUNG MYRTLE** *and* **YOUNG WINIFRED.** *A song comes on.*)*

YOUNG MYRTLE. I love this song.
I feel so fresh. So, woke!

YOUNG MYRTLE. I don't know if that's a correct use of "woke" Winifred.

YOUNG WINIFRED. Aw flippidy jippidy!

EUGENE. Bark bark bark!

---

*A license to produce *Winifred and Myrtle Go to High School* does not include a performance license for any third-party or copyrighted music. Licensees should create an original composition or use music in the public domain. For further information, please see Music Use Note on page 3.

YOUNG WINIFRED. I'm just glad we're enjoying this time. Who knows how long it'll last?

End of Play

AROUND 2

James Anthony Tyler

AROUND 2 was first produced by Keen Company at Theatre Row in New York City from May 11-13, 2018. The performance was directed by Estefania Fadul, with assistant direction by Kyle Michael Yoder, scenic design by An-Lin Dauber, costume design by Karen Boyer, lighting design by Kate August, and sound design by Käri Berntson. The production stage manager was Steven Hernandez. The cast was as follows:

EVELYN	Natalya Gammon
JAYCEON	Samuel Taveras
DEB	Petra Brusiloff
ANDY	Jacob Bergman
EAMON	Noor Alnashash
MING	Ella Rosalind Couchman
RAUL	Alex Espinal-Martinez
ALISA	Irene Lauren Colon-Nava
ISAAC	Reign Casillas
MRS. ROBINSON	Safiya Christian

CHARACTERS

EVELYN – 17, female, African American

JAYCEON – 17, male, mixed race: African American and white

DEB – 17, female, white American

ANDY – 17, male, white American

EAMON – 17, female, Pakistani American

MING – 17, female, Chinese American

RAUL – 17, male, Mexican American

ALISA – 17, female, mixed race: Native American and Mexican

ISAAC – 17, male, Dominican American

MRS. ROBINSON – 37, female, African American

NEWS ANCHOR – Any adult age, any gender, any race. Lines can be recorded or performed live.

Scene One

(Around 6:29 p.m.)

*(In darkness, we hear the voice of a **NEWS ANCHOR**.)*

NEWS ANCHOR. Alright, take a look at this, uhh what a sight. This is Manhattan and you see the Empire State Building right there. That's our news helicopter that's flying over Manhattan right now. History will be made in the United States of America.

*(Lights up on a classroom. **MRS. ROBINSON** stands across from **EVELYN**.)*

MRS. ROBINSON. How do you expect me to tolerate...

EVELYN. Mrs. Robinson...

MRS. ROBINSON. Tolerating this...

EVELYN. Can I just say...?

MRS. ROBINSON. Evelyn *Evelyn*. Let me finish?

EVELYN. Alright. Finish.

MRS. ROBINSON. Thank you. Evelyn, you're smart. Everyone looks up to you, and...

EVELYN. Raul is the most popular, if he would have run for president...

MRS. ROBINSON. I'm not done! ...You know right from wrong... Tolerating Raul's behavior sends the wrong message.

EVELYN. Mrs. Robinson, he means well.

MRS. ROBINSON. Meaning well means that you don't post the stuff that he did. It's hateful. It's disgusting.

EVELYN. But she defends Trump. Said if she could vote...

MRS. ROBINSON. It doesn't matter. Just because she's for a candidate that he doesn't like, that's not an excuse for *his* behavior. Online, she's been called every name under the sun. Downright mean emojis and GIFs sent to hurt her feelings.

EVELYN. Raul was just upset.

MRS. ROBINSON. Not an excuse.

EVELYN. I really don't believe that his intentions were to hurt her. I think he was just trying to wake her up.

MRS. ROBINSON. Aren't there better ways?

(Silence.)

And how can you be sure that his intentions weren't to hurt her?

EVELYN. Excuse me?

MRS. ROBINSON. How can you be so sure?

EVELYN. Because he's my friend that I've known since the first day of freshman year.

MRS. ROBINSON. Well, I know him too. I've been his teacher twice. U.S. Government and World History. I've seen the way he debates firsthand. It's not always nice.

EVELYN. People just debate like...*mean* sometimes.

MRS. ROBINSON. Evelyn...

EVELYN. Have you been paying attention to the campaigns? Trump and Hillary are both going for blood.

MRS. ROBINSON. That's different.

EVELYN. How?

(A beat.)

MRS. ROBINSON. Okay, you have a point, but at this school we have standards. In this club we have standards. This government club was created so students can come together and discuss politics in a healthy way. You know the goal is to listen to each other's differences and to let those differences exist while still treating each other humanely. Posting "racist troll" on someone's social media is not humane. He knows it's wrong to encourage people to attack Deb on social media. She doesn't deserve that. She's the treasurer of this club.

EVELYN. And he's the vice president.

MRS. ROBINSON. Not for much longer if he doesn't apologize.

EVELYN. Wait a minute!

MRS. ROBINSON. Evelyn, you're the president of this organization, and I expect you to take action.

EVELYN. What are you getting at?

MRS. ROBINSON. As the club advisor I must, and am, firmly suggesting that you have Raul make a speech at tomorrow's club meeting where he apologizes to Deb.

EVELYN. I can't make him do that.

MRS. ROBINSON. If you can't make him do it then you have to demand his resignation.

EVELYN. This is crazy.

MRS. ROBINSON. It's far from crazy. It's the right thing to do. Whoever wins the election tonight...

EVELYN. Hillary...

MRS. ROBINSON. We both hope... Whoever wins will be the president of all Americans. You are the president of all of the students in this club and you have an obligation to look out for ALL of them. Even the ones who have opinions that you don't agree with.

EVELYN. So, this is an ultimatum?

MRS. ROBINSON. I don't like doing this, but I have to look out for everyone.

EVELYN. I make Raul apologize *publicly*, or I make him resign?

MRS. ROBINSON. Correct.

EVELYN. He's not going to say he's sorry, and I can't make him resign.

MRS. ROBINSON. Then you'll have to terminate him from being VP.

EVELYN. Whoa! Are you really putting me in this position?

MRS. ROBINSON. Raul's actions put you in this position.

EVELYN. Not cool. And you *had* to do this on the day that I watch a woman become president of my country for the first time. Me, Ming, Eamon, Alisa…it's all that you've heard us talking about this last week. No, not even just last week. You've heard us talking about this since last spring.

MRS. ROBINSON. Oh come on! You know me well enough to know that I'm not trying to ruin this night for you. The principal of the school knows. Sent me an e-mail this morning, because he was made aware of Raul's social media post last night. He wants this resolved by the start of school on Thursday.

EVELYN. So, you don't have a choice?

MRS. ROBINSON. I don't.

EVELYN. What if you and I both go to Principal…

MRS. ROBINSON. It won't work. What I am advising has to be the way things are. Tomorrow Raul is either giving a formal apology or choosing to no longer be a member.

EVELYN. He's applying to all of the Ivys. Being VP of this club all but ensures that he's accepted. I can't do anything that will possibly ruin that.

MRS. ROBINSON. Listen, I know that this is challenging, but I believe, *I know* that you can convince Raul to do the right thing.

EVELYN. This is really the worst.

Scene Two

(Around 7:22 p.m.)

*(In darkness, we hear the voice of the **NEWS ANCHOR**.)*

NEWS ANCHOR. Let's start with an early projection. Donald Trump is the winner in West Virginia. Donald Trump will carry that state with five electoral votes. Trump gets another state, West Virginia. We have another key race alert right now. Too early to call, too early to call in North Carolina...

*(Lights up on a classroom. **EVELYN**, **MING**, **ALISA**, and **DEB** watch the TV. **EVELYN** switches the TV off.)*

EVELYN. It's still hours away until this thing is decided, so no need for us to sit in front of the TV worried.

MING. Where are the boys? And where's Mrs. Robinson?

EVELYN. Mr. Robinson called her cell, she stepped out right before you walked in. Raul, Isaac and Andy went to the bodega for snacks. Jayceon is in another room doing trig work.

ALISA. Evelyn, your man is O.D. That trig work is extra credit. He already has the highest score in the class.

EVELYN. Don't hate on Black excellence.

ALISA. Half Black excellence. He's only half.

EVELYN. Whatever!

(They laugh.)

ALISA. And I'm not worried about this election. Hill got this! We know we're going to witness the first lady president in the history of our nation, so I'm not worried at all.

*(Points at **DEB**.)*

She should be worried.

(Silence.)

MING. *(To* **DEB.***)* Are you worried?

DEB. No. Yes. I don't know to be honest.

ALISA. Deb, I don't understand how you're not backing a woman.

DEB. I have to explain this to you *again*, Alisa?

EVELYN. Wait... Stop! ...You know what I've been thinking. We've been a part of this club since our freshman year. In every meeting there is a topic of discussion that we debate and the conversations are great, but...I think tonight...we just watch the results. No need for discussion. No need for debate. We watch in silence and...you know...whatever happens happens.

MING. The president of the Government Club is suggesting that we don't discuss politics...that we don't discuss government?

EVELYN. Just for tonight.

ALISA. Why? You're protecting Deb? Because she should be able to defend...

DEB. I do defend.

ALISA. ...Her beliefs and reasons for supporting a male chauvinist pig!

DEB. I have a right to my opinion.

MING. "She's a nasty woman. Such a nasty woman." That's okay with you?

DEB. They were having a heated debate.

ALISA. Sounds like your answer is yes.

DEB. In a heated debate sometimes people say things that they don't mean.

EVELYN. That's true.

MING. Evelyn, does she have *you* defending Donald Trump now?

EVELYN. No way! I'm not defending that orange ugly cow.

ALISA. Then what's up with you being all like, "That's true"?

EVELYN. I'm just saying that in a heated debate people can sometimes say things that they don't mean. Deb, it's just like what Raul put on your Facebook wall.

MING & ALISA. *(Laughing.)* Racist troll.

DEB. That's not funny!

(Silence.)

EVELYN. He didn't mean it.

DEB. He did. Don't even try it.

EVELYN. Listen to me...

DEB. No, you listen... I've already talked to Mrs. Robinson, and I know that Raul is going to have to apologize or not be a member of this club.

EVELYN. Not be vice president.

DEB. Not be vice president or a member in any kind of way. It hasn't been an entire twenty-four hours and I've received over 500 DMs. I couldn't even get through them all. The ones that I did open were threats. Violent threats. Physical threats.

EVELYN. WHAT? I didn't know that... No wonder why Mrs. Robinson...

ALISA. Deb, what the hell do you expect when you support a racist asshole? Now that you get a few threats we're supposed to care about your white girl tears.

DEB. It was more than a few.

ALISA. Whatever! How can you sit in here knowing that Raul is Mexican and knowing that he has family members here who are illegal immigrants... How can you sit here and be proud to vote for the host of *The Apprentice*?

EVELYN. We're all seventeen so we're technically not voting for anyone.

ALISA. You know what I mean, and she knows what I mean. Deadass, I wanna know how you can vote for him knowing he's been talking foul about Mexicans...?

DEB. He's just saying those things. He's not really going to build a wall...and my dad needs a job. You all know that his engineering firm laid him off two years ago and he's been looking for a permanent job ever since. We need change.

MING. Oh, just say it's because Raul dumped you for Eamon. He dumps you, the white girl and starts going out with Eamon, the Pakistani Muslim girl. After that you start coming to this club every week bragging about how Trump is the better candidate? It's only because you're all up in your feelings.

DEB. That's not true.

ALISA. It is.

EVELYN. Enough!

(A beat.)

Alisa, Ming, I need you both to chill.

MING. Evelyn, she doesn't deserve your defense. You didn't hang with her freshman and sophomore year and even the beginning of last year. You only hung with her a few times when her and Raul were together, so you don't know that she wasn't popping none of this Republican stuff before.

DEB. For your information, I've always been Republican.

ALISA. No, you got all Republican at the end of this summer after Raul dumped you. If you were really Republican you'd be anti-abortion.

EVELYN. STOP IT! In this club we can have our differences, but we have to always be cordial. Always!

DEB. Exactly! And that's why I deserve, and better get, an apology from Raul.

Scene Three

(Around 9:41 p.m.)

*(In darkness, we hear the voice of the **NEWS ANCHOR**.)*

NEWS ANCHOR. Right now we have a major projection in the battle for the United States Congress. We can now project that Republicans will keep control of the House of Representatives. Now Speaker Paul Ryan's fight to maintain the Republican majority is paying off...

*(Lights up on a stairwell where **EVELYN** sits with **JAYCEON**.)*

EVELYN. Letting the GOP keep the House! People in this country are crazy. NYC is the only sane city. I never want to leave.

JAYCEON. But you're going to, right? For college? With me?

EVELYN. No... Jayceon...

JAYCEON. Am I hearing things right? Did you... NO?! ...I thought I heard...my girlfriend...

EVELYN. What I'm trying to say...

JAYCEON. ...Tell me "no" that she is not going to California to attend Stanford with me? That's what I thought I heard.

(Silence.)

EVELYN. I don't know what I'm saying.

JAYCEON. You are going to college, right?

EVELYN. I'm going to college. I'm going to Stanford. I'm going to California with you.

JAYCEON. Good.

(They kiss.)

EVELYN. What if he wins?

JAYCEON. Don't even think like that.

EVELYN. How do I tell Raul to apologize to Deb if Donald Trump wins and becomes our president?

JAYCEON. Why would you ever tell Raul anything like that?

EVELYN. Because Mrs. Robinson is making me.

JAYCEON. Hold up, I'm confused.

EVELYN. Mrs. Robinson said that Raul's post on Deb's Facebook page was wrong and that now people are threatening her.

JAYCEON. Good.

EVELYN. No, it's not good. About two hours ago I thought I was going to have to pull Ming and Alisa off of her.

JAYCEON. If I was in the room and it started popping off where Ming and Alisa are giving Deb's wack ass the business, I would just turn my head the other way.

EVELYN. You're too smart to sound so dumb.

JAYCEON. And you sound like you're cool with a Becky that supports a KKK member getting into the White House. I mean, just this weekend you and I were watching that video of Trump pointing to that brotha and saying, "Look at my African American!" You okay with that?

EVELYN. You know I'm not.

JAYCEON. Well, that's what it sounds like when you talk about making Raul apologize to Deb.

EVELYN. Jayceon, I'm in a tough spot. Mrs. Robinson told me that I either get Raul to apologize or I tell him that he's no longer VP of the club.

JAYCEON. She can't make you do that.

EVELYN. She's the club advisor.

JAYCEON. Evelyn, I'm telling you, you're NOT going to do this.

EVELYN. Don't tell me what to do.

JAYCEON. Are you using your brain?

EVELYN. See, this is why I didn't want to date a Black man with a white momma.

JAYCEON. That's really below the belt.

EVELYN. In middle school, and my first two years in this high school, white girls stayed talking down to me like I couldn't possibly have a functioning brain. Your mother has done the same thing.

JAYCEON. Leave my momma out of this.

EVELYN. I'm not letting my boyfriend treat me like that too.

JAYCEON. Look, chill. I'm sorry. It's just...Raul will never apologize.

EVELYN. He'll have to.

JAYCEON. He's the most bullheaded Taurus that I've ever known, and you know that I've known him practically my entire life. First grade! Even after being friends that long I can tell you that I don't think I've ever seen him apologize for anything. Even when he is dead wrong he doesn't do it.

EVELYN. Well, there's a first time for everything.

JAYCEON. This shouldn't be the first because this time he's right.

EVELYN. So, you think it's right for him to post "racist troll" on Deb's page and then tell folks to have a "petty party"?

JAYCEON. If that person supports someone who calls Mexicans rapists and says he's going to build a wall on the border then yeah...hell yeah...I say it's absolutely right.

EVELYN. I'm your girlfriend.

JAYCEON. Why are you saying something that we both know?

EVELYN. Because I want you on my side... I have to ask you...

JAYCEON. Nonono! I know you're not about to ask me...

EVELYN. Jayceon, if you could just talk to him and get him to...

JAYCEON. I'm not doing that.

EVELYN. It's going to look really bad if he has to resign from the club. How do you think all of those Ivy League schools are going to look at this?

JAYCEON. They won't have to look at anything if you just stand up to Mrs. Robinson. Tell her that you are not going to force Raul to do anything *and* you're not going to stop him from being VP of the club.

EVELYN. Jayceon…

JAYCEON. Can't you just tell her that?

EVELYN. What if Deb was your sister?

JAYCEON. Don't go there.

EVELYN. If Deb was your sister and Raul wrote that on her wall you wouldn't stand for this.

JAYCEON. Since Raul and Eamon… Yo, Deb is just jealous…

EVELYN. Oh, sexism! So now she's the crazy jealous ex-girlfriend?

JAYCEON. Are you really turning on my best friend over her? You said all of that stuff about white girls, but now you want to go all hard and make my best friend apologize to that Taylor Swift victim playing white girl. Put yourself in Raul's shoes and think about the fear that he has lived with for basically all of his life. His dad was offered a construction gig in Long Island last year and he couldn't work the job for fear that he could be sent away from his fam. Deb is stupid and entitled and doesn't deserve an apology. I'm not asking Raul anything.

Scene Four

(Around 11:59 p.m.)

(In darkness, we hear the voice of the **NEWS ANCHOR**.*)*

NEWS ANCHOR. Let's take a look at the electoral college map, see where it stands right now, the all-important electoral college map. Donald Trump is ahead. He has 232 electoral votes compared to Hillary Clinton's 209 electoral votes. So, you need 270 to become the President of the United States.

> *(In the classroom,* **JAYCEON, DEB, EAMON, MING, ALISA, MRS. ROBINSON,** *and* **EVELYN** *all sit and watch TV. After a moment,* **EAMON** *taps* **EVELYN** *and they both walk out of the room and into a hallway.)*

EAMON. What were you and Jayceon talking about earlier?

EVELYN. Raul.

EAMON. Why?

EVELYN. I know that you know, and it's cool.

EAMON. What?

EVELYN. I know my boyfriend. As my mom says, "Jayceon stays spilling the tea." He's a talker. It's one of the things that I love about him.

EAMON. Listen, he was just...

EVELYN. You don't have to cover for him. I know that he talks. He's not afraid to express the way he feels. It's cool.
Raul is his best friend. You're dating Raul and I know that my boyfriend probably ran to you and Raul as soon as I was done talking to him. He's real loyal to his b.f.

EAMON. He's right about... She doesn't deserve an apology.

EVELYN. Does she deserve threats?

EAMON. Does Raul and his family deserve to be deported?

EVELYN. No. You know I don't think that.

EAMON. But Deb does. She's okay with their lives being threatened so if she's taking some heat on social media...so be it.

EVELYN. People are sending her messages that aren't nice.

EAMON. Okay, people say spicy stuff online. That's just words. What could happen to my boyfriend's family should be your real concern.

EVELYN. Eamon...

EAMON. I know you and I aren't the best of friends, but we've always got along and I feel like I know you well enough to know that you're not losing sleep over Deb. Just think about not *just* who she is supporting but the type of ideas that she seems to be okay with. Remember last month when you and I were talking about how Trump talks about Black neighborhoods like all that goes on in them is crime? I didn't have a chance to tell you then, but I wanted to tell you that my family moved here when I was seven and that we have lived in Harlem since then. We both know it's majority Black people...well, I think it still is...anyway, we love our neighborhood and we always loved our neighbors and there is a lot more than just crime going on where I live.

EVELYN. I know.

EAMON. I doubt if Deb does though. She's just as bad as Trump.

  (Silence.)

EVELYN. Did you know some guy threatened to knock her teeth out?

EAMON. Did you know that my dad was attacked and was in the hospital for three weeks after 9/11? He came here to set things up for my mom, me, my sister and brother. He was driving a taxi... I know, stereotypical Pakistani job in New York...

  (They chuckle.)

A white guy. My dad said the guy was wearing a suit and was around thirty years old. Dragged him out of the car and then all of a sudden my dad felt punches and kicks and my dad said he didn't know how many guys were attacking him but it was definitely more than one. My old man is from Pakistan. Not Afghanistan! Not Iraq! That didn't matter... She supports hate.

EVELYN. Aren't we doing the same? If we stand by Raul's actions?

(RAUL, ISAAC, and ANDY enter.)

ISAAC. Evelyn, Eamon! Andy thinks me and Raul from the same country.

ANDY. That's not true! Don't listen to him.

ISAAC. He keeps talking about the "Latino vote" like we're all the same.

ANDY. I just said that most Latinos are going to vote for Hillary.

ISAAC. But I told you that a lot of Mexicans are going to vote for Trump and you were acting like you don't believe me.

RAUL. Isaac, don't talk about my people.

ISAAC. I'm not talking about your people. I'm just saying that some of them are voting for Trump.

RAUL. But most aren't.

ISAAC. Aiight. Take your panties out your butt, dude.

EVELYN & EAMON. You're being sexist.

ISAAC. I'm sorry. I'm not trying... Y'all know I love women! And hey, my Dominican ass uncle is voting for Trump, which I think is crazy as hell, but he keeps saying Trump is a man of God. My uncle is crazy-Catholic, like goes to church every day. I told him, "Trump ain't no man of God," but my uncle doesn't listen to me and he's voting for that over-tanned asshole. All I'm saying is that, just like your people *(Points at* **ANDY**.*)* aren't all the same, my people aren't either.

ANDY. I get it.

ISAAC. Do you?

ANDY. You know I do.

ISAAC. Alright, then no more generalizations.

ANDY. Right. Yeah. No more generalizations.

ISAAC. But it is true that my people got that rhythm and can dance and yours ain't got none and can't!

> (**ISAAC** *does an upbeat bachata step.*)

ANDY. That's not true.

EVELYN. Isaac, Andy, can you two go in the classroom so I can talk to Eamon and Raul.

ISAAC & ANDY. About what?

> (**EAMON** *shoots them both a look.* **ISAAC** *and* **ANDY** *rush into the classroom.*)

EVELYN. Raul...

RAUL. I'm not apologizing to her.

EAMON. Babe, let Evelyn speak.

RAUL. I already know what she's going to say. Deb has done disgusting things before...and now this Trump garbage. No way will I say sorry to her, and I need you to have my back, not make me give up VP of the club.

EVELYN. Raul, but Mrs. Robinson...

RAUL. Nah! ...Jayceon is like my brother, so you and me we're like family. Last year when you became Pres and I became VP, we said we'd always have each other's back. You got mine?

EVELYN. I have to do what's right.

RAUL. Is having the back of the girl who looks up to a white supremacist right?

EVELYN. I guess...it's not...but... Raul. I'll think about your stance on this... And I'll let you know...but I do have your back.

Scene Five

(Around 2:00 a.m.)

(A spotlight on **EVELYN**.*)*

EVELYN. And we watched in disbelief. Together. The votes came in. A mountain so steep. Too steep. Way too steep for her to climb. At least on this night. Red red red red red red red. Blue. More red red red red red red red red red red red red red red red. Blue. Not enough blue. And then Van Jones from a desk in a CNN newsroom talked about Muslims being afraid. Van Jones called it a whitelash against a changing country.

Van talked. Jayceon cried. Van talked. Eamon cried. Van talked. Andy cried. Van talked. Alisa cried. Van talked. Isaac cried. Van talked. Ming cried. Van talked. Raul cried. Van talked… Deb cried… I cried…and I cried…and I cried.

> *(The lights rise and all of the* **STUDENTS** *and* **MRS. ROBINSON** *watch the TV. Everyone has tears in their eyes. Some of the* **STUDENTS** *embrace.)*
>
> *(***MRS. ROBINSON** *turns off the TV. She stands.)*

MRS. ROBINSON. I just want to make sure one more time, that everyone called their parents to let them know that you're still at the school, and that they're okay with you being here this late. I know that I already received permission slips from each parent, but I still want to be sure that being here so late is okay. Everyone did that, call or text, right?

> *(All of the* **STUDENTS** *nod yes. A beat.)*

It's two a.m., so we shouldn't stay much longer. Maybe another thirty minutes and we're all out of here.

> *(Silence.)*

Should we talk?

> *(Silence.)*

MRS. ROBINSON. Okay. We don't have to talk here, but if we don't can we make sure that we find time to talk with friends, with parents or other trusted family members. However you feel, you should find someone who you feel safe with expressing your feelings. You all know that I'm here. My door is always open to you all.

EVELYN. *(Points at DEB.)* Why is she crying?

MRS. ROBINSON. Evelyn.

EVELYN. It's what you wanted, right?

DEB. Evelyn…

EVELYN. DON'T SAY MY NAME LIKE WE'RE FRIENDS!

>   *(JAYCEON walks over and tries to comfort EVELYN.)*

JAYCEON. Bae, let me walk you home.

EVELYN. I don't want to go home.

JAYCEON. It's going to be alright.

EVELYN. I want to know why she's crying.

DEB. I'm crying because…we're all crying.

EVELYN. But you got what you wanted, didn't you?!

MRS. ROBINSON. EVELYN, STOP IT RIGHT NOW! YOU'RE THE LEADER OF THIS CLUB.

EVELYN. Maybe I shouldn't be.

JAYCEON. Bae, you don't know what you're saying.

EVELYN. I do! Maybe the world is showing us how things have to be, saying only guys are meant to lead.

MING. Evelyn, you know you're good.

ALISA. You're the best president this club has ever had.

ISAAC. Evelyn, you gotta keep your head up. You run this.

EVELYN. She doesn't deserve an apology, Mrs. Robinson.

MRS. ROBINSON. We can talk about this some other time.

EVELYN. I want to talk now!

MRS. ROBINSON. Jayceon, please…

>   *(JAYCEON tries to escort EVELYN out.)*

JAYCEON. Come on, Ev, let's go ahead and…

EVELYN. GET – YOUR – HANDS – OFF – ME!

>(**EAMON** *walks over to* **EVELYN**.)

EAMON. Evelyn, let's walk together.

EVELYN. People who did that to your dad. They're out there. Tonight they won.

EAMON. Maybe.

EVELYN. Look at this election... The same thing that happened to your dad can happen to you, to me, to most in this room.

EAMON. And it could have happened before this election. We can't let it change us. Change the good we're meant to do... Should we...walk home together?

>(**EVELYN** *nods yes. They head to the door.*)

It's not over.

EVELYN. You still think she'll win?

EAMON. I don't know but I'm saying, I'm not going to just sit back and let that fool just do whatever. It's not over.

EVELYN. Yeah, it's not. Won't change the good we're meant to do.

>(**EVELYN** *and* **EAMON** *exit.*)

JAYCEON. I'm going to walk with them.

>(**JAYCEON** *exits. They all stand in silence.*)

MRS. ROBINSON. Just want to make sure again, does anyone want to talk?

RAUL. Fuck this shit!

>(**RAUL** *rushes out.* **DEB** *runs out to catch him.* **RAUL** *runs to the stairwell,* **DEB** *is right behind him.*)

DEB. Raul!

RAUL. Yo, you've caused enough...

DEB. Why would you tell people to attack me?

RAUL. Why would you go behind my back and... Why?

DEB. You're too young to be anyone's father.

RAUL. You know that wasn't right.

DEB. It's my body.

RAUL. Tell that to your next president.

DEB. No, I'm telling you. How do you sit up and act like you're so liberal but you try to control my body?

RAUL. The party that you support are the ones trying to control women's bodies, not me. I just wanted...

DEB. It was my decision.

RAUL. So, you don't think I get any say?

DEB. That's the reason? It's not politics. Because of my decision you think that you had the right to post those awful words.

RAUL. I'm not sorry.

Scene Six

(Around 12:00 p.m.)

(A spotlight on **EVELYN**.*)*

EVELYN. She speaks. A concession speech. Tells us our constitutional democracy demands our participation, not just every four years, but all the time. She told us to keep advancing the causes and values we all hold dear. She spoke about making our economy work for everyone, not just those at the top.

She spoke of breaking down all the barriers that hold any American back from achieving their dreams. She said, "We believe that the American dream is big enough for everyone." And I believed. Again. I believed... I believe... There is work to do.

> *(Lights up on the classroom.* **EVELYN** *and* **RAUL** *stand across from each other.)*

EVELYN. Remember last spring when you brought Deb to my house?

RAUL. I didn't bring Deb to your house.

EVELYN. You did.

RAUL. No, that's not how that went down.

EVELYN. She was with you and Jayceon.

RAUL. Jayceon invited her over.

EVELYN. Are you serious?

RAUL. Yeah.

EVELYN. Oh yeah, I think that is how it went down.

RAUL. Yeah, I wasn't going with her yet.

EVELYN. Okay, yeah, yeah, yeah. You remember I didn't like her?

RAUL. For real?

EVELYN. We were watching those interviews of Rihanna on YouTube.

RAUL. Oh yeah.

EVELYN. And I was looking at Deb like, "I do not like you."

RAUL. I remember Jayceon kept telling you, "Fix your face."

EVELYN. I was ready to go off on her.

RAUL. What did she do to you?

EVELYN. She kept making those comments about Rihanna's accent.

You don't remember that?

RAUL. She always makes comments about people's accents.

EVELYN. She really thought she was being slick.

RAUL. One time her and I had this huge argument because she kept trying to do my dad's voice.

EVELYN. That's so disrespectful.

RAUL. She apologized.

EVELYN. Okay, I guess that's cool… I guess.

RAUL. I kinda made her though because I was mad and ready to end it. She didn't want us to be over so she did what was good.

    (Slight pause.)

EVELYN. That's what you have to do.

RAUL. We're back to you trying to make me apologize?

EVELYN. The world is full of people who have opinions that you and I disagree with. You and I have opinions on certain things that we don't agree on. That doesn't mean that we have the right to belittle people online and try to get others to do the same. How would you feel if someone did actually hurt her?

RAUL. This isn't cool. One minute you say you have my back and then the next minute you flipping the script.

EVELYN. Did you listen to the concession speech?

RAUL. I don't care about a speech.

EVELYN. Do you care about trying to get things right?

RAUL. Do you care that she went and had an abortion behind my back?

EVELYN. Raul…

RAUL. Don't try to pretend like you don't know. We both know that Jayceon is the biggest talker in the world.

EVELYN. You cannot trust him with your secrets.

RAUL. Never trust him with those. I knew he'd tell you.

(A beat.)

EVELYN. I'm sorry she hurt you.

RAUL. I'm cool.

EVELYN. No, you were with someone and then she turned out to be something you didn't know at all. When you got with her I would have sworn she was a Democrat.

RAUL. I mean, she did… To keep it all the way real, she did tell me that she was a Republican when we first started going out.

EVELYN. And you kept going with her?

RAUL. This is before she was into Trump.

EVELYN. I wish Jayceon would start acting all red state on me. He knows he better not.

RAUL. Oh, he knows he better not.

(A beat.)

So, you understand where I'm coming from.

EVELYN. Understanding doesn't make it right. You see, where I'm coming from? "So let's do all we can to keep advancing the causes and values we all hold dear…

(A beat.)

I love her concession speech. I also loved what Michelle Obama said at the convention, "When they go low, we go high." You went low and now I need you to go high.

(A beat.)

You know that the meeting starts after school, around two, once everyone seems to have gathered and are in their seats. Listen to me, I'm being very clear, we either start the meeting with a speech of you apologizing to Deb or I start it with announcing that you are no longer VP and no longer a member of the Government Club. It's your decision.

RAUL. Got it.

EVELYN. So, I'll see you at the meeting?

RAUL. If me, you, Jayceon and Eamon go to Mrs. Robinson...

EVELYN. Raul...

RAUL. Isaac and Andy would have our back...

EVELYN. Raul...

RAUL. I think Ming and Alisa would too.

>   *(A long beat.)*

EVELYN. We're not going to Mrs. Robinson.

RAUL. So, that's it?

EVELYN. That's it... Will I see you around two?

>   *(**RAUL** and **EVELYN** take a deep breath as they look each other in the eyes as the lights fade.)*

End of Play

THE CARIBBEAN QUEEN

Music by Salomon Lerner
Book and Lyrics by
Jamie Cowperthwait

THE CARIBBEAN QUEEN was first produced by Keen Company at Theatre Row in New York City from May 11-13, 2018. The performance was directed and choreographed by Ilana Ransom Toeplitz, with associate direction by Jenna Rossman, musical direction by Salomon Lerner, scenic design by An-Lin Dauber, costume design by Karen Boyer, lighting design by Kate August, and sound design by Käri Berntson. The production stage manager was Cinthia Chen. The cast was as follows:

SAM . . . . Leanora Octavia Tapper
SAM'S MOM. . . . . .Fatou Tall
SAM'S DAD . . . . Nijewel Hall
CAPTAIN FRED / PIRATE CAPTAIN FREDERICK . . . Marc Andrew De Jesus
FIRST MATE SANDY / PIRATE SECOND MATE SANDY . . . .Max M. Grinnell
SECOND MATE SHELLY / PIRATE FIRST MATE SHELLY. . . . . Kiara Jorge
SIRI / PIRATE SIRI . . . . Marina Davey
ENSEMBLE. . . . . Abigail Meyer, Jael Margarita Hoyos, Valencia Heaven Motta, Gabriella Derke

CHARACTERS

SAM – 16-18
SAM'S GRANDMA
SAM'S GRANDPA
CAPTAIN FRED / PIRATE CAPTAIN FREDERICK
FIRST MATE SANDY / PIRATE SANDY
SECOND MATE SHELLY / PIRATE SHELLY
SIRI – the voice of the Apple iPhone
PIRATE SIRI – 16-18
CREW 1, 2, 3 & 4 / PIRATE CREW 1, 2, 3 & 4
YOUNG PASSENGER

Any references to a character's gender in the script are based on the first production. All characters may be played by any race or gender and pronouns may be changed accordingly.

SETTING

The main deck of the Caribbean Queen – a massive cruise ship that becomes a pirate ship when Sam travels back in time.

Scene One

[MUSIC NO. 01 "THE QUEEN OF THE OLD CARIBE"]

*(The **CREW** of the Caribbean Queen along with **CAPTAIN FRED**, **FIRST MATE SANDY**, and **SECOND MATE SHELLY** welcome the new passengers as they board. **SAM**, **GRANDMA**, and **GRANDPA** enter. The **CREW** bestows fruity drinks, beach towels, and sun hats on them, mists them, etc. **GRANDMA** is thrilled by the attention. **GRANDPA** holds a brochure and checks it throughout the song and scene. **SAM** alternates between being embarrassed by her grandparents and absorbed in her phone.)*

[Note: The word "Caribe" in this song is pronounced "Cuh-reé-bay" with the accent on the second syllable.]

CREW 1 & 2.
　THROW OUT YOUR TROUBLES AND WORRIES
CREW 3 & 4.
　ABANDON YOUR CARES ON THE BREEZE
FIRST MATE SANDY.
　WE SAVED YOU A FIRST-CLASS SEAT
SECOND MATE SHELLY.
　AND STOCKED UP YOUR FIRST-CLASS SUITE
CREW 1, 2, 3 & 4.
　WITH RED BULL AND CAMEMBERT CHEESE
CREW 1.
　TREAT THE WHOLE FAM TO A SUNSET
CREW 2.
　GOLD OVER AQUA-MARINE

CREW 3.
RELAX AT THE TIKI BAR
CREW 4.
DRINK UP FROM A MASON JAR
SANDY & SHELLY.
AND TAKE IN THE TROPICAL SCENE
CAPTAIN, MATES & CREW.
YOU'RE ON THE QUEEN OF THE OLD CARIBE
THE QUEEN OF THE OLD CARIBE
YOU SIMPLY MUST TASTE THE CUISINE
ABOARD THE OLD CARIBBEAN QUEEN

> (**GRANDMA** *dances to the music, getting into the island vibe.* **GRANDPA** *has his nose in the brochure and sways his hips gamely.* **SAM** *rolls her eyes.*)

GRANDMA. Feel the rhythm. The rhythm of the islands!

GRANDPA. *(Looking up from the brochure.)* Your grandmother can really dance, can't she?

GRANDMA. Sam, we're so thrilled to have you with us on this cruise vacation. There's nothing like spending time with our granddaughter.

> (**GRANDMA** *and* **GRANDPA** *surround* **SAM** *as they dance.* **SAM** *forces a smile and goes back to her phone.*)

GRANDMA. You can put your phone away for the rest of the trip.

GRANDPA. You'll be so busy having fun you won't even miss it.

> (**SAM** *smirks as if to say, "Yeah right."*)

GRANDMA.
PLAY MINI GOLF UNDER BLACKLIGHTS
GRANDPA.
BUY YOUR COLOGNE DUTY-FREE
GRANDMA.
IF YOU WANT TO PARASAIL

GRANDPA.
>YOU WON'T HAVE TO SHARE A SAIL

GRANDMA & GRANDPA.
>THE SHIP HAS ONE HUNDRED AND THREE

ALL EXCEPT SAM.
>YOU'RE ON THE QUEEN OF THE OLD CARIBE
>THE QUEEN OF THE OLD CARIBE
>A VACAY SO SWEET AND SERENE
>ABOARD THE OLD CARIBBEAN QUEEN

GRANDMA. Look at that view.

>*(To* **SAM***.)* Sam, do you see that gorgeous ocean view?

SAM. *(Still absorbed in her phone, not looking up.)* Uh-huh, sure Grandma…

>*(She strikes a model pose and takes a selfie.)*

Hashtag nonchalant.

GRANDMA. *(To* **SAM***.)* Maybe you can make some friends here on the boat.

SAM. Thanks, Grandma, but I don't need any more friends. If you haven't noticed, I'm VERY popular.

GRANDPA. In my day, we met friends at the roller rink. Now it's some kind of app where you post pictures? I don't get it.

GRANDMA. It's called "socialized media," dear. It's all the rage with the kids these days. There's MyFace, iPads, and "texting"… I can't keep track of all the new "apps." There's even a woman who lives in your phone and answers all your questions. Her name's "Alexa."

SAM. For the record, I'm posting to my followers on Instagram and the woman who "lives in my phone" is called "Siri."

GRANDPA. I've got a woman who lives with me and answers all my questions. She's called my wife!

SAM. *(Into her phone.)* Siri, how do I describe Instagram to my grandfather?

SIRI. *(Offstage.)* Instagram is a mobile, desktop, and internet-based photo-sharing application with over eighty million active users.

GRANDPA. I hate to break it to you, Sam, but this boat only holds five thousand two hundred and eighty-six people. You'll have to leave your eighty million friends on land.

GRANDMA. Ask Siri what happens if you leave your phone in the cabin for the week. I'm sure she'll tell you to go out and live a little.

SIRI. *(Offstage.)* Please don't leave me behind. I'll be so lonely.

GRANDMA. Goodness, Siri. I didn't realize you were so social.

(**SAM** *goes back to taking selfies.*)

SAM. *(Narrating her Instagram caption into her phone.)* Hashtag cruise ship life.

GRANDPA. *(Reading brochure.)* Oh my goodness, look at this. The boat has a pirate plank.

GRANDMA. A pirate plank?! Sam, doesn't that sound thrilling?

SAM. If that's your idea of fun.

GRANDPA. It says right here, "Not long ago these waters were filled with pirates. Some say, you can still see their ships on the horizon at sunset if you look hard enough. Don't miss our latest attraction. The Pirate Plank! Now you can walk the plank like Yellowbeard himself."

GRANDMA. I'm sure it's just harmless fun. What do you say, Sam?

SAM. No thanks.

Scene Two

GRANDPA. Come on, Sam, not even to see your grandpa walk the plank?

SAM. I'm good. Thanks.

GRANDMA. *(Disappointed.)* Okay. We'll see you at dinner then.

SAM. Mmkay, byeee.

> (**SAM** *turns away from* **GRANDMA** *and* **GRANDPA** *and goes back to her phone.*)

[MUSIC NO. 02 "ALL THESE FRIENDS (IN MY PHONE)"]

> (**GRANDMA** *and* **GRANDPA** *fade into the background. We see them in silent, slow-motion action interacting with the* **CREW** *while* **SAM** *sings. They eat, drink, shop, play golf, and do everything the ship has to offer.*)

SAM.
 I "LIKE" YOU
 I "LIKE" YOUR HAIR
 I "LIKE" YOUR STYLE AND THE CLOTHES YOU WEAR
 YOU POST PICTURES ON MY FEED OF EVERYTHING YOU OWN
 AND THAT'S WHY WE'RE BEST FRIENDS
 IN MY PHONE

> (**SAM** *takes a selfie and posts it.*)

 YOU "LIKE" ME
 YOU "LIKE" MY SHOES
 YOU MAKE ME FEEL LIKE I'M IN THE NEWS
 WHO NEEDS BLACKLIGHT MINI GOLF OR DUTY-FREE COLOGNE
 WHEN I HAVE TONS OF FRIENDS
 IN MY PHONE?

> (**SAM** *takes another selfie and posts it.*)

 BECAUSE I HAVE SO MANY FRIENDS
 I'M NEVER ON MY OWN

> I NEVER LEAVE THE HOUSE WITHOUT
> MY CHARGER AND MY PHONE
> IT'S ALL RIGHT HERE IN MY PHONE!
>
> THEY "LIKE" ME
> I "LIKE" THEM TOO
> WHAT ELSE IS LEFT FOR GOOD FRIENDS TO DO?
> I MAY BE FLOATING OUT TO SEA BUT I AM NOT ALONE

>> (**GRANDMA**, **GRANDPA**, *and the* **CREW** *are in limbo formation, holding a bar and waiting for Sam.*)

GRANDPA. Hey, Sam, come do the limbo with us!

GRANDMA. How lowwwwwwww can you go?

>> (**SAM** *turns away from the limbo scene and back to her phone.*)

SAM.
> CUZ I'VE GOT ALL THESE FRIENDS
> IN MY PHONE

>> (**CAPTAIN FRED**, **FIRST MATE SANDY**, *and* **SECOND MATE SHELLY** *move downstage. We see them looking over at Sam and her grandparents. They confer briefly and seem to agree on something before breaking formation.*)

CAPTAIN FRED. Ahoy, sailors. I'm your captain, Captain Fred.

GRANDPA. Nice to meet you, Captain Fred.

FIRST MATE SANDY. And I'm First Mate Sandy.

SECOND MATE SHELLY. And I am Second First Mate Shelly.

FIRST MATE SANDY. (*To* **SHELLY**.) You are the second mate, Shelly. There's only one first mate on a ship.

SECOND MATE SHELLY. That is a matter of opinion.

FIRST MATE SANDY. I am the first mate. You are the second mate.

SECOND MATE SHELLY. Again. Matter of opinion.

CAPTAIN FRED. I hope you're enjoying your stay on the Caribbean Queen.

GRANDMA. We're having a wonderful time.

GRANDPA. Doing the limbo fixed my back. This is our granddaughter, Sam.

> (**SAM** *is still absorbed in her phone.*)

CAPTAIN FRED. Pleased to meet you, Sailor Sam.

> (**SAM**, *in her phone, barely acknowledges* **CAPTAIN FRED**.)

GRANDMA. Captain Fred, I wanted to ask you something.

FIRST MATE SANDY. All questions can be directed to me, the first mate.

SECOND MATE SHELLY. And if the first first mate doesn't know the answer the second first mate always does.

FIRST MATE SANDY. Shelly!

(*To* **GRANDMA**.) Don't pay any attention to her.

GRANDPA. It says in the brochure that there used to be pirates in these waters.

FIRST MATE SANDY. *(Perhaps too cheerfully.)* Does it say that?

SECOND MATE SHELLY. Sure does. Right on page five.

FIRST MATE SANDY. *(Annoyed.)* Shelly.

(*To* **GRANDMA**.) And what is your question?

GRANDMA. *(Meekly.)* Are there *still* pirates in these waters?

CAPTAIN FRED. *(Asserting himself, laughing way too hard.)* Oh, ho, ho, no, no, no, no, no. Is that what you're worried about? No, no, no, no, no, no, no, no, no, no, no, no. There are NO pirates in these waters.

CREW 2. *(Passing by.)* Not unless you believe in time travel.

FIRST MATE SANDY. Which we don't!

GRANDMA. I guess we're safe then.

GRANDPA. Great! Captain Fred, if you'll point us in the direction of the Pirate Plank, we've got some swashbuckling to do.

CAPTAIN FRED. *(Forcefully.)* You can't walk the plank.

GRANDMA. It says right here, "Walk the Pirate Plank just like the olden days."

CAPTAIN FRED. The Pirate Plank is closed.

FIRST MATE SANDY. What the captain's saying is that the Pirate Plank attraction has been closed indefinitely due to some recent...irregularities.

SECOND MATE SHELLY. (*Using air quotes.*) "Irregularities."

FIRST MATE SANDY. Shelly!

GRANDMA. Was there an accident?

FIRST MATE SANDY. (*Laughing way too hard.*) No, no, no, no, no, no, no, no, no, no, no, no, no, no. Nothing mind-blowing and mysterious happens if you walk the Pirate Plank. It's just closed for now.

GRANDMA. Why are you crossing your fingers?

FIRST MATE SANDY. What? This? This is just an old sailors' superstition. At sea, we cross our fingers when we're telling the truth.

SECOND MATE SHELLY. (*Using air quotes.*) "The truth."

FIRST MATE SANDY. I will hurt you, Shelly!

CAPTAIN FRED. Now that that's settled, you go have yourselves some fun.

GRANDMA. Thank you, Captain Fred.

(**FIRST MATE SANDY** *and* **SECOND MATE SHELLY** *exit.*)

GRANDPA. Okay, then. The Pirate Plank is out. What next?

GRANDMA. Why don't we all go to the mall. You can buy yourself some new swim trunks and Sam and I will shop for sundresses. And maybe afterward, we can go to the casino. I want to try playing craps!

GRANDPA. Sounds like a plan!

SAM. K. Have fun. I'll meet you at dinner.

(**GRANDMA** *and* **GRANDPA**, *disappointed in Sam, turn to exit.*)

SAM. (*To* **GRANDMA** *and* **GRANDPA**.) Wait!

(**GRANDMA** *and* **GRANDPA** *turn hopefully.* **SAM** *snaps a picture of them and narrates her Instagram caption.*)

SAM. *(Narrating.)* "Grandma and Grandpa going to the mall. Hashtag how cute are old people?"

> (**GRANDMA** *and* **GRANDPA**, *upset, exit.* **SAM** *tries to post to Instagram but is not getting any reception. She tries again. Still no reception.)*

SAM. *(Desperate.)* Captain Fred! I'm not getting any reception.

CAPTAIN FRED. Yeah, that'll happen. There's very little service on the boat.

SAM. I won't be able to post anything all week?

CAPTAIN FRED. Nope.

SAM. *(Distraught to the point of near-insanity.)* No, Captain Fred, no! No, no, no, no, no, no, no, no!

> *(Pause.)*

No.

CAPTAIN FRED. *(Pretending to keep a secret that he has every intention of telling Sam in the end.)* Alright. I really shouldn't tell you this because we encourage passengers not to use cell phones on the boat but, heck... I guess I can let you in on a little secret... No, I shouldn't say it...

SAM. What? What were you going to say?

CAPTAIN FRED. Legend has it...there's WiFi on this boat.

> (**SAM** *gasps.*)

SAM. What?!

CAPTAIN FRED. I can't say any more than that.

SAM. You have to tell me! What's the network name? What's the password?!

CAPTAIN FRED. Well, you didn't hear this from me but there's a network called "Frederick's mirror" and nobody knows why it's there. Some say it's a ghost... WiFi network!

SAM. I see it! It's right here. What's the password?!

CAPTAIN FRED. You definitely didn't hear this from me but I've heard, and again, this is just a legend, that the password is "arrrrrrggh one-eight-two-zero." That's six "r"s in "arrrrrrggh."

SAM. Yes! It's working! But I'm not even getting one bar. The signal's so weak. I can't post anything! What do I do?

CAPTAIN FRED. Well, you ABSOLUTELY did not hear this from me but *(Stage whisper.)* you get a better signal over by the Pirate Plank.

[MUSIC NO. 02A "WALKING THE PLANK"]

SAM. Yes! Thank you!

CAPTAIN FRED. Whatever you do, don't go too close to the edge of the plank...because it's CLOSED! ...But do go there... I mean, DON'T... But do...but don't...but do... If you want a stronger signal on the ghost WiFi network.

SAM. Thank you, Captain Fred! Thank you. Thank you!

> (**CAPTAIN FRED** *exits.* **SAM** *moves toward the Pirate Plank in search of a better signal.*)

SAM. Oh, come on baby. Come to Mama. One bar!

> (*She has come upon the entrance to the Pirate Plank. There is a big barrier with a sign reading "DUE TO...'IRREGULARITIES,' THE PIRATE PLANK IS CLOSED" fastened to it, but* **SAM**, *so close to having enough signal to post her photo, ducks under the barrier.*)

SAM. Yes, yes, yes. Two bars! Still sending? Still sending? Post! No, no. So close!

> (**SAM** *realizes that to get enough signal she's going to have to walk out onto the plank. She steps out.*)

SAM. *(Looking at her phone.)* Yes! Three bars! Almost... almost...almost...yes!!

> (*Losing her balance,* **SAM** *screams and falls. Magical time warp music plays as she falls*

through time and space.* When the lights come up she is asleep on the deck of the Caribbean Queen, which is now a pirate ship. The **PIRATE CREW** *enters and sings but does not notice her.)*

---

*This music is not included in the score. A license to produce *The Caribbean Queen* does not include a performance license for any third-party or copyrighted music. Licensees should create an original composition or use music in the public domain. For further information, please see Music Use Note on page 3.

Scene Three

[MUSIC NO. 03 "THE QUEEN OF THE OLD CARIBE (REPRISE)"]

PIRATE SHELLY. All right, ye scurvy pirates, Captain Frederick'll be on deck at sundown to inspect the ship after last night's storm.

(*Pointing at* **PIRATE SANDY**.) First Mate Sandy here is in charrrrge of the cleanup.

PIRATE SANDY. Actually, First Mate *Shelly* is in charrrrge of the cleanup and everybody knows what happens if Captain Frederick ain't happy with yer work...

> (*The* **PIRATE CREW**, *including* **SHELLY** *and* **SANDY**, *scurry about, working as they sing.*)

PIRATES 1 & 2.
PULL OUT YER WASHRAGS AND SOAPSUDS

PIRATES 3 & 4.
WE'RE PIRATES AFLOAT ON THE SEAS

PIRATE SANDY.
YOU CAN BET THAT WE'LL RING YER NECK

PIRATE SHELLY.
JUST AS SOON AS WE SWAB THE DECK

PIRATES 1, 2, 3 & 4.
ARRR CAPTAIN'S A HARD MAN TO PLEASE

PIRATE SHELLY & PIRATE SANDY.
GET TO WORK!

ALL PIRATES.
ON THE QUEEN OF THE OLD CARIBE
THE QUEEN OF THE OLD CARIBE
THE DECK MUST BE SPARKLING AND CLEAN
ABOARD THE OLD CARIBBEAN

> (*The* **PIRATE CREW** *continues to work, exclaiming "Arggggghhh!" loud and often.* **PIRATE SHELLY** *and* **PIRATE SANDY** *place a large ornamental mirror in its stand.*)

PIRATE SHELLY. Careful now, Sandy. Everything must be in its place for the inspection. And this mirror...oh, this mirror is a priceless beauty.

PIRATE SANDY. Ye think I don't know that?

PIRATE 1. Captain Frederick tells us every chance he gets about how he looted it from the British Navy himself.

> (**PIRATE SANDY** *touches the mirror admiringly.*)

PIRATE SHELLY. Don't touch it!

PIRATE SANDY. I'm not touching it. Yer touching it!

PIRATE SHELLY. I am not, ye lazy land crab!

> (**PIRATE SHELLY** *and* **PIRATE SANDY** *have a brief shoving match that culminates in them almost breaking the mirror. They are both terrified at the prospect of breaking it.*)

PIRATE SHELLY. Whoa!

PIRATE SANDY. Easy does it!

> (*They rescue the mirror and both breathe a sigh of relief when it is safe.*)

PIRATE SANDY. And we're done.

PIRATE 2. We've still got to swab the deck –

PIRATE 3. – And coil the hawsers –

PIRATE 4. – And mend the rigging.

PIRATE SANDY. What? I'm too tired. I'm quitting.

PIRATES 1, 2, 3 & 4. If yer quitting, we're quitting too!

PIRATE SHELLY. Well, I sure ain't swabbing the entire deck meself.

PIRATE SANDY. It's yer responsibility. Yer the first mate!

PIRATE SHELLY. I'm not the first mate. Yer the first mate!

PIRATE SANDY. No, you are!

PIRATE 1. Captain Frederick will have us all walking the plank no matter who's the first mate.

PIRATE 2. It's impossible. The plank's closed.

PIRATE 3. What do ye mean, the plank's closed? How do ye close a pirate plank? It's just a piece of wood.

PIRATE 2. The captain walked a British Navy admiral off the plank yesterday and the feller disappeared.

PIRATE 3. Of course he disappeared. He sank like a stone.

PIRATE 4. No, he never hit the water.

*(The **PIRATES** all gasp in unison.)*

PIRATE SHELLY. *(Spying **SAM**.)* Hold on. Who's this?

PIRATE SANDY. Up, ye ragamuffin.

PIRATE SHELLY. Must be a stowaway who came above deck during last night's storm.

PIRATE SANDY. *(Rousing **SAM**.)* Up, up. Enough loitering. So, rough seas drove ye aboveboards last night, did they?

SAM. Where am I?

PIRATE SHELLY. Shoulda asked yerself that before you stowed away. Don't play innocent with me, ye little thief. I may be a pirate but at least I work for me passage.

PIRATE SANDY. I bet ye think piratin's all sword-fighting and treasure hunting? Hah. It's harrrrrrrrd work.

PIRATE 4. And we should know...

PIRATES 1, 2, 3 & 4. We've been cleaning all day.

PIRATE SANDY. The true nature of piratin' is harrrd work. Most people never learn that!

SAM. First Mate Sandy!

PIRATE SANDY. How dare ye call me first mate!
*(Pointing to **SHELLY**.)* There's yer first mate.

PIRATE SHELLY. If ye call me first mate one. more. time!

SAM. What happened? Why are you all dressed like pirates?

PIRATE SANDY. Shut yer mouth, stowaway!

SAM. Very funny. Can you get me an aspirin and a Diet Coke?

PIRATE SHELLY. Stop jabbering or we'll make ye walk the plank.

PIRATES 1, 2, 3 & 4. *(To **PIRATE SHELLY**.)* We told ye, the plank's closed.

PIRATE SHELLY. *(To* **PIRATE SANDY.***)* Well, then we'll shoot her and roll her overboard.

SAM. Why is everyone being so mean to me? I want to speak to Captain Fred immediately and also if you can get me a little thing of sunscreen for my face that'd be great. Mmkay, thanks!

> (**SAM** *tries to reach for her phone in her pocket to check social media while she waits for her Diet Coke and sunscreen, but* **PIRATE SANDY** *or one of the other* **PIRATES** *stops her with a hand on the shoulder.*)

PIRATE SANDY. Oh, you'll meet Captain Frederick all right. But I'll warn ye, he hates stowaways! Come with us.

PIRATE SHELLY. Hold on a minute. Let's make the kid clean the ship.

PIRATE SANDY. Ahhhhhh, I see what yer saying. We'll make the kid the first mate!
(To **SAM.***)* Here, start swabbing this deck. And when you're done, coil the hawsers and mend the mainsail. And then we'll see how much ye like piratin', ye little layabout.

> (**PIRATE SHELLY** *shoves a mop into* **SAM***'s hand.* **PIRATE SHELLY** *and* **PIRATE SANDY** *stare at* **SAM***, who stands helpless.*)

PIRATE SHELLY & PIRATE SANDY. Well, what are ye waiting for?! Start swabbing!!

SAM. How dare you talk to me that way?

ALL PIRATES. How dare ye talk to US that way!

PIRATE SHELLY & PIRATE SANDY. Get to work!

> (**PIRATE SANDY** *and* **PIRATE SHELLY** *exit.*)
>
> (**PIRATE SIRI** *enters, carrying a book, but* **SAM** *doesn't see her.*)
>
> (**SAM** *starts to mop, then considers rebellion, then sees the hopelessness of her situation. She*

> *slumps down and begins to cry. She reaches into her pocket and pulls out her phone.)*

SAM. *(Talking to her phone.)* Siri, where am I?

PIRATE SIRI. You're on the deck of the Caribbean Queen, the most feared pirate brigantine in all the tropics.

SAM. Siri, what happened?

PIRATE SIRI. You've been captured by my father, Captain Frederick Bottomly. This is his ship, the Caribbean Queen and if you know what's good for you, you'll start swabbing this deck.

> (**SAM** *turns around and is astonished to see that* **PIRATE SIRI** *is a real person.)*

SAM. Who are you?

PIRATE SIRI. I'm Siri. Who are you?

SAM. I'm Sam.

PIRATE SIRI. Hello, Sam. What are you doing on our ship?

SAM. Why is everyone talking about pirates and all dressed up like olden times?

PIRATE SIRI. What do you mean "olden times"? The Caribbean Queen is a very modern ship.

SAM. I mean "olden times"! You know, like it's the eighteen hundreds.

PIRATE SIRI. It IS the eighteen hundreds!

SAM. What?!

PIRATE SIRI. I said it IS the eighteen hundreds!

SAM. You mean...we're in the past?

PIRATE SIRI. What?!

SAM. You're telling me we're in the past?

PIRATE SIRI. No, I'm telling you we're in the present.

SAM. No.

PIRATE SIRI. Yes.

SAM. Two-thousand-eighteen is the present.

PIRATE SIRI. Whoa, you're from the future?

SAM. No, I'm from the present!

PIRATE SIRI. No, you're from the future.

SAM. You're from the past!

PIRATE SIRI. I'm from THE PRESENT!!

>   *(Beat.)*

>   If you're not from the future, then what was that object you were talking into?

SAM. My phone? What about it?

>   (**PIRATE SIRI** *is in awe of the phone as a totally foreign object.*)

PIRATE SIRI. It's so beautiful. What does it do?

SAM. I use it for taking pictures and posting them to social media so my friends can see.

PIRATE SIRI. You have friends?

SAM. Of course.

PIRATE SIRI. Where are they?

SAM. I have like hundreds of friends from literally all over the world.

PIRATE SIRI. Whoa. And you talk to them through that?

SAM. Yeah, all the time.

PIRATE SIRI. That must be wonderful.

SAM. Everybody has friends.

PIRATE SIRI. Yeah, I guess you're right.

SAM. *(Being judgemental.)* Are you saying you have *no* friends?

PIRATE SIRI. I didn't say that.

SAM. You acted super surprised when I told you I have a lot of friends.

PIRATE SIRI. There aren't any other kids on this boat, so...

SAM. Surely you haven't spent your whole life on this boat.

PIRATE SIRI. Surely I have.

SAM. What?

PIRATE SIRI. I was born right over there on the deck.

SAM. But you must have friends at school.

PIRATE SIRI. I don't go to school.

SAM. Whoa, I can't even imagine how you live.

PIRATE SIRI. It's not like I'm alone.

SAM. *(Sarcastic.)* Right, because you have Sandy and Shelly. Yay.

PIRATE SIRI. I have my mother.

SAM. Your mother?

PIRATE SIRI. That's right, my mother. She's my closest friend in the whole world. We do practically everything together.

SAM. Then…where is she now?

PIRATE SIRI. Oh, right now, she's not here…she's in Barbuda… I think. She's a very successful artist. She travels a lot for work.

SAM. My grandparents always want to be best friends with me. It drives me crazy. They are so extra!
(Pointing to **PIRATE SIRI**'s *book.)* What's that?

PIRATE SIRI. Nothing. It's a book.

SAM. Cool cover. Can I see it?

PIRATE SIRI. Um…okay.

    *(***PIRATE SIRI*** hands* **SAM** *the book.* **SAM** *reads the cover.)*

SAM. "*The Merry Mother's Guide to Pirating: The Secret to Accomplishing Any Task on a Pirate Ship in Just One Easy Step*. Now with a brand-new index." This book seems kind of weird.

    *(***PIRATE SIRI*** grabs the book back.)*

PIRATE SIRI. It is NOT weird! My mother wrote this book and drew all the pictures herself!

SAM. Whoa! I didn't know you were going to be so EXTRA about it.

PIRATE SIRI. I'm not "extra," whatever that means. Not everyone has "hundreds of friends from literally all over the world" like you.

PIRATE SANDY. *(Offstage.)* I don't hear any work happening up there!

PIRATE SHELLY. *(Offstage.)* Don't make the first mate come up there and feed ye to the sharks.

PIRATE SANDY. *(Offstage.)* Cuz that first mate would be Shelly!

SAM. They're going to kill me and I have no idea how to clean a ship. Can you help me or SOMETHING?

PIRATE SIRI. Oh, yeah, sure… I'd love to but…

SAM. Look, I'm sorry I said you were extra. Please help me.

PIRATE SIRI. Yeah, okay, about that…

SAM. What's the matter?

PIRATE SIRI. *(Blurting out.)* I don't know how to clean a ship.

SAM. What?! I thought you were born "right over there on the deck."

PIRATE SIRI. To be honest, when I'm not reading, I spend most of my time traveling with my mother.

Scene Four

SAM. *(Having an idea.)* Wait a minute! Your book! Give me that thing!

[MUSIC NO. 04 "ASK A FRIEND"]

(**SAM** *grabs the book and reads the cover.*)

"The Secret to Accomplishing Any Task on a Pirate Ship in Just One Easy Step."

(To **PIRATE SIRI.***)* What's the one easy step, Siri? What's the one easy step?!

PIRATE SIRI. I'm sure it's in there somewhere.

SAM. Haven't you read this book a thousand times?

PIRATE SIRI. Yes. No. I don't know.

SAM. What do you mean you don't know?

PIRATE SIRI. I can't read!

SAM. What else can't you do, huh? Because you might as well tell me now before they throw me overboard and I get EATEN BY SHARKS!

PIRATE SIRI. You don't have to be so "EXTRA" about it.

PIRATE SANDY. *(Offstage.)* Don't make me come up there and run ye through with my sword!

SAM. Give me that.

(**SAM** *flips through the book.*)

Here! Page forty-six…"How to Swab a Deck."

PIRATE SIRI. Oh, so THAT'S what that says.

SAM.
 WHEN YOU'RE HANDED A MOP AND A PAIL OF SUDS
 WHEN THE GREASE AND THE GRIME SEEP INTO YOUR
  DUDS I'D RECOMMEND
 YOU ASK A FRIEND

What does that even mean?

PIRATE SIRI. I don't know but I've been looking at this picture my whole life. It's all right there in the illustrations.

(They swab the deck.)

Done! Now the ropes?

> (**SAM** *flips through the book.*)

SAM. Here. Page sixty-four.
> WHEN YOU'RE KNEE-DEEP IN TANGLES AND YOU'RE COILING ROPE
> WHEN YOUR ARM'S GETTING TIRED AND YOU'RE LOSING HOPE
> YOU WON'T OFFEND
> JUST ASK A FRIEND

I swear this book is so extra!

PIRATE SIRI. *(Looking at the picture.)* It is not extra! Look!
> YOU PASS THE ROPE TO ME
> MAKING SURE THE END IS FREE
> AND THAT'S THE WAY A ROPE SHOULD BE!

> *(They coil the ropes.)*

Now let's mend the mainsail.

SAM. Huh, this actually seems to be working.

> *(She has found the right page in the book.)*

> WHEN YOU'RE STUCK WITH A NEEDLE AND SOME SEWING THREAD
> AND THE WEIGHT OF THE WORLD'S HANGING OVERHEAD
> DON'T BREAK OR BEND

PIRATE SIRI. Let me guess...
> JUST ASK A FRIEND

SAM.
> YEAH!

PIRATE SIRI.
> YOU PASS THE THREAD TO ME

SAM.
> YOU SEND IT BACK

PIRATE SIRI.
> AGAIN MAKES THREE

PIRATE SIRI & SAM.
> AND THAT'S THE WAY

PIRATE SIRI.
>A SAIL SHOULD BE

>>*(They hoist the sail in an instant and it billows in the wind.)*

SAM.
>FLYING FREE!

PIRATE SIRI.
>WE SWABBED A DECK

SAM.
>WE COILED SOME ROPE

PIRATE SIRI.
>WE FIXED A SAIL

SAM.
>CUZ WE ARE DOPE!

PIRATE SIRI. Yeah, we're dope?

SAM.
>WHEN YOU'RE TRAPPED IN THE PAST AND YOU CAN'T GO BACK

SIRI.
>WHEN THE WATER'S STORMY AND THE SKY IS BLACK

SAM.
>IT'S NOT THE END

PIRATE SIRI & SAM.
>JUST ASK A FRIEND!

>>*(**SAM** throws her arm around **PIRATE SIRI** and pulls her close, taking a selfie of the two of them. **SAM** shows the picture to **PIRATE SIRI**.)*

PIRATE SIRI. Wow! It's like a magical mirror!

SAM. It's called a "selfie."

>*(**PIRATE SANDY** and **PIRATE SHELLY** enter assuming the work has not been done.)*

PIRATE SANDY. That's it! We're throwing ye overboard.

PIRATE SHELLY. Yer headed to the bottom of the sea. Giant sharks have to eat too!

> (**PIRATE SANDY** and **PIRATE SHELLY** realize the work has been done.)

PIRATE SANDY. Hold on a minute! They've done it!

PIRATE SHELLY. How'd ye do it?!

PIRATE SANDY. What's yer secret?

SAM. Just um...asked a friend.

PIRATE SHELLY. Well, I'll be blasted! Ye mean, if I've got a problem I can't solve, I can ask me friend Sandy here?

PIRATE SIRI. Yup, she'll help you out.

PIRATE SHELLY. Arrrgh, I love ye, Sandy

PIRATE SANDY. Arrrgh, I love ye too, Shelly.

> (**PIRATE SANDY** and **PIRATE SHELLY** hug and "Arrrgh" a lot.)

PIRATE SANDY. *(To* **SAM.***)* Look at ye... Yer a real pirate now.

PIRATE SHELLY. Now ye know that the true nature of piratin' is harrrrd work! Most people never learn that.

PIRATE SANDY. Ye look different, too.

PIRATE SHELLY. Ye've got a glow about ye.

PIRATE SANDY. Take a look at yerself in Captain Frederick's mirror.

> (**PIRATE SANDY** and **PIRATE SHELLY** lead **SAM** to Captain Frederick's mirror to show her her reflection. **SAM** looks at herself, pleased with what she sees.)

PIRATE SIRI. Careful with that!

> (**SAM** grabs the mop and poses as a hard-working pirate. Her poses are no longer helpless "model" poses. Now, they are active and full of energy.)

PIRATE SHELLY. I know, I know it's yer dad's prized possession.

SAM. Siri, come pose with me.

> (**PIRATE SIRI** joins **SAM**. The two of them pose in joyful, powerful poses. **PIRATE SHELLY** and

PIRATE SANDY *move the mirror around in accordance with* **SAM**'s *wishes.)*

SAM. *(To* **PIRATE SHELLY** *and* **PIRATE SANDY**.*)* Can you move back a little?

PIRATE SIRI. *(To* **PIRATE SHELLY** *and* **PIRATE SANDY**.*)* Watch the edge.

SAM. Little farther.

PIRATE SIRI. Just be careful not to get too close to the edge.

SAM. And one more big step back.

PIRATE SIRI. Watch where you're stepping!

> *(***PIRATE SHELLY** *and* **PIRATE SANDY** *take a big step back. They run into the ship's railing. The mirror goes overboard. We hear a loud splash.* **PIRATE SANDY** *and* **PIRATE SHELLY** *look at* **PIRATE SIRI**, *then at each other, and freak out.* **PIRATE SIRI** *looks stricken.* **PIRATE 2** *enters.)*

PIRATE 2. Look sharp, mateys. Captain Frederick's coming.

> *(***PIRATE SHELLY** *and* **PIRATE SANDY** *freak out even more.* **PIRATE CAPTAIN FREDERICK** *enters.)*

PIRATE CAPTAIN FREDERICK. Ahoy, ye worthless dogfish, it's inspection time! I shiver when I think of the lousy work ye've done in the past and I'm certain this time will be every bit as hideous, invidious, and downright piteous as last ti– well, it actually looks pretty good so far. Perhaps yer not a bunch of spineless sea urchins after all.

PIRATE SANDY. That's right. Aye aye, captain! Me friend Shelly here and me worked with no rest.

PIRATE SIRI. Hey!

> *(***PIRATE CAPTAIN FREDERICK** *turns and sees* **PIRATE SIRI**.*)*

PIRATE CAPTAIN FREDERICK. Run along, Siri. Daddy's pirating.

PIRATE SIRI. But, Father, it's just that...

PIRATE CAPTAIN FREDERICK. Just that what?

PIRATE SIRI. It's not true. Sandy and Shelly didn't do all the work.

PIRATE CAPTAIN FREDERICK. Well, who did then?

PIRATE SIRI. *(Pointing at* **SAM.***)* She did!

PIRATE CAPTAIN FREDERICK. What?!

PIRATE SIRI. That's right. Sam did all the work.

PIRATE CAPTAIN FREDERICK. Who is Sam and why is she on my ship?

PIRATE SHELLY. She's a stowaway, Captain.

PIRATE SIRI. She's not a stowaway. She's my friend. And she cleaned the entire ship.

SAM. But I couldn't have done it without Siri. She taught me how to swab, and coil, and mend everything.

PIRATE CAPTAIN FREDERICK. *(To* **PIRATE SHELLY** *and* **PIRATE SANDY.***)* Is this true?

PIRATE SHELLY. Erm…um…well, yes.

PIRATE SANDY. But we only tried to take credit because we know how much ye hate stowaways.

PIRATE SHELLY. So…really, it was to protect ye.

PIRATE SANDY. I guess ye could say, we did it out of love.

PIRATE SHELLY. I think that's / true.

PIRATE CAPTAIN FREDERICK. Enough!! I don't want to hear another word out of either of ye. Sam and Siri, ye've done an admirable job cleaning the ship. Frankly, Siri, I didn't know ye had it in ye. Perhaps ye'll make a real pirate someday after all. Now, I'd like to inspect meself before dinner. First Mate Shelly, fetch me my mirror, you know, the one I single-handedly looted from the British Navy.

PIRATE SHELLY. Aye, Captain, but I'm not the first mate.

(Everyone winces.)

PIRATE CAPTAIN FREDERICK. *(Keeping a lid on his anger.)* Well then… First Mate *Sandy*, fetch me my mirror, you know, the one I single-handedly looted from the British Navy.

PIRATE SANDY. *(Very hesitantly.)* I would, Captain...but I also am not the first mate.

> *(Everyone fidgets nervously.)*

PIRATE CAPTAIN FREDERICK. Is there *anyone* on this ship who can fetch me my mirror, the one I single-handedly looted from the British Navy?

PIRATE SHELLY. *(Interrupting and fending off the* **CAPTAIN***'s anger.)* So good news! The mail boat came and delivered that new set of rubber stamps you ordered from the Amazon!

PIRATE SANDY. Wow, who would have thought they could deliver ye a new set of stamps from the Amazon in just nine months. It's an amazing time in which we live.

PIRATE CAPTAIN FREDERICK. *(Seeing through their ploy and drawing his sword in a rage.)* Fetch me my mirror NOW!

PIRATE SIRI. Father.

PIRATE CAPTAIN FREDERICK. In a moment, Siri.

PIRATE SIRI. Father!

PIRATE CAPTAIN FREDERICK. What is it, Siri?

PIRATE SIRI. We don't have the mirror.

> *(The* **PIRATES** *gasp.)*

And it's my fault.

> *(The* **PIRATES** *gasp.)*

I knocked it overboard.

> *(The* **PIRATES** *gasp.)*

I'm sorry, Father. I'll go back to staying out of everyone's way now.

PIRATE CAPTAIN FREDERICK. Siri, my girl, I was right about ye all along. Ye aren't meant to be a real pirate. Now run along, child.

> *(***PIRATE SIRI** *turns away from her father.* **SAM** *goes to her and hugs her. The two hold hands and, without the other pirates seeing,* **SAM** *gives* **PIRATE SIRI** *her cell phone.)*

SAM. Captain Frederick...

PIRATE CAPTAIN FREDERICK. *(Extremely irritated.)* Not now.

SAM. Siri has something for you.

PIRATE CAPTAIN FREDERICK. *(Angry.)* I said not now! Can't you see I'm doing pirate stuff?!

> (**PIRATE SIRI** *holds out Sam's cell phone.*)

PIRATE SIRI. I have something to give you, Father.

PIRATE CAPTAIN FREDERICK. *(Irate.)* What in the name of Neptune are you talking about, Siri?!

PIRATE SIRI. It's even better than your prized mirror.

PIRATE CAPTAIN FREDERICK. *(Interested but still wary.)* It's quite beautiful...but what is it?

PIRATE SIRI. It's a magical, mystical mirror.

PIRATE CAPTAIN FREDERICK. *(Annoyed.)* What does it do?

SAM. *(Jumping in.)* Here, I'll show you.

> (**SAM** *shows* **PIRATE CAPTAIN FREDERICK** *how to take a selfie. He is astonished to see himself on the screen.*)

PIRATE SIRI. It's you!

PIRATE CAPTAIN FREDERICK. Why, it is me! I've never seen anything like it.

> (**PIRATE CAPTAIN FREDERICK** *has transformed into a complete dandy, utterly captivated by his own image. Whatever fearsomeness he had is gone.*)

I look ravishing. The color. The contrast. My dashing chin. My piercing eyes.

SAM. You have great cheekbones. Have you ever thought about modeling?

PIRATE CAPTAIN FREDERICK. I have actually. May I take another?

SAM. Of course. You can take as many as you like.

> (**PIRATE CAPTAIN FREDERICK** *takes more pictures and delights in each one.*)

PIRATE CAPTAIN FREDERICK. Siri, my child, this is magnificent. You simply must tell me where you got it.

PIRATE SIRI. I... I... I...

SAM. She looted it from the British Navy!

PIRATE CAPTAIN FREDERICK. She what?!

SAM. Tell him, Siri.

PIRATE SIRI. That's right. During your parley with Admiral Wellington last week –

PIRATE CAPTAIN FREDERICK. *(Remembering fondly.)* He thought he could negotiate my surrender.

PIRATE SIRI. I boarded the ship in the middle of the night and walked right into the admiral's chambers.

PIRATE CAPTAIN FREDERICK. Past the guards? But how?

SAM. She's quick. And quiet. Like a ninja! Sorry, just ignore me.

PIRATE SIRI. I took the magical mirror right off his bedside table. The admiral must have had a few too many rum and tonics that night because he never stopped snoring.

PIRATE CAPTAIN FREDERICK. *(Sniffling with pride.)* She looted it from Admiral Wellington himself. Me own daughter. A real thief! I didn't know I could be this happy. Come over here, Siri. Let's get a picture of both of us together. I want to commemorate yer first day as a REAL pirate. Now ye know that the true nature of piratin' is adventure! Most people never learn that.

PIRATE SANDY. *(Under his breath.)* The true nature of piratin' is harrrd work.

PIRATE SHELLY. *(Under her breath.)* Most people never learn that.

PIRATE CAPTAIN FREDERICK. Excuse me?!

PIRATE SANDY & PIRATE SHELLY. Nothing, Captain.

> (**PIRATE CAPTAIN FREDERICK** *places his hat upon* **PIRATE SIRI***'s head and takes a picture of both of them together.*)

PIRATE CAPTAIN FREDERICK. Arrrggghhh, look at the two of us. Like father like daughter.

(**PIRATE SIRI** *breaks away happily and moves to* **SAM**. **PIRATE CAPTAIN FREDERICK** *remains transfixed and oblivious to all those around him and takes selfie after selfie in various poses.*)

PIRATE SIRI. What's the matter?

SAM. I can't stay here any longer. I have to go.

PIRATE SIRI. Okay. I'll ask my father for your phone back.

SAM. No! That's your gift to him.

PIRATE SIRI. How will you live without your phone?

SAM. I'll be fine. It's not like a person can't live without a cell phone. But first, before I leave, let's take one last selfie.

(**SAM** *reaches for her phone only to realize it's not there.*)

Oh...

PIRATE SIRI. That's what I'm talking about. I know how important that phone is to you. Without it, how will you talk to all your friends?

SAM. Siri, I should probably tell you something.

PIRATE SIRI. You're right, you can just talk to them at school.

SAM. No, Siri –

PIRATE SIRI. Besides, they won't want to hear about some old pirate ship.

SAM. Siri, stop! Listen to me! I don't...actually have any friends.

PIRATE SIRI. What are you talking about?

SAM. I don't actually know any of those people, the ones in my phone.

PIRATE SIRI. What about school? You don't need a phone to see your friends at school.

SAM. School? Are you kidding? I have no friends at school!

PIRATE SIRI. What?

SAM. I get so nervous around people. I try to talk but I can never remember what to say and whenever I try to tell a joke no one laughs. And this fall, one of the popular girls at school called me ugly on Instagram and five hundred people liked her post.

PIRATE SIRI. But you're not ugly at all.

SAM. Thanks. I pretended not to see it but I did. Ever since then, I just spend all my time on social media pretending I'm really popular.

PIRATE SIRI. I promise I'll NEVER say anything bad about you on Instagram…and not just because I don't know what Instagram is.

SAM. Thanks. I'm sorry I said your mom's book was "extra." It's a beautiful book and she sounds like an amazing woman. You're lucky to have a real friend like her.

PIRATE SIRI. Sam –

SAM. And she's family too, so you guys will be friends for life.

PIRATE SIRI. Sam, I have to tell you something.

SAM. To think of you being jealous of me when you've got your mom –

PIRATE SIRI. Sam, please! I have to tell you something. My mom's not in Barbuda. And we're not best friends.

SAM. What do you mean?

PIRATE SIRI. My mother was lost at sea when I was two years old. I found this book in a chest in my dad's cabin. I keep it and look through the pictures and try to figure out what she must have been like…

Scene Five

(**SAM** *hugs* **PIRATE SIRI**.)

SAM. Siri, I'm so sorry.

PIRATE SIRI. Thanks.

(**SAM** *takes the book from* **PIRATE SIRI**.)

SAM. I'll tell you what your mother was like. She was an amazing woman. Look here...
(*Reading.*) "Dear Siri, if someone is reading you this inscription, then you have learned that the true nature of pirating is friendship. Most people never learn that."

[MUSIC NO. 05 "TWO BEST FRIENDS (WITH NO PHONE)"]

(**SAM** *and* **PIRATE SIRI** *hug.*)

I LIKE YOU

PIRATE SIRI.

I LIKE YOU TOO

SAM.

THERE'S SO MUCH ELSE THAT TWO FRIENDS CAN DO

PIRATE SIRI.

WE MAY BE FLOATING OUT AT SEA

PIRATE SIRI & SAM.

BUT WE ARE NOT ALONE
CUZ WE ARE TWO BEST FRIENDS
WITH NO PHONE

PIRATE SIRI. Don't go.

SAM. I have to. My grandparents must be worried sick about me. As far as they know, I'm lost at sea...like your mom. I'm so sorry that happened to you. And now I see why I could never do that to Grandma and Grandpa.

PIRATE SIRI. I'll miss you.

SAM. I'll miss you too.

(**SAM** *steps up onto the Pirate Plank to head back to the future.*)

SAM. Bye, everyone. I have to go now.

ALL PIRATES. *(Ad-lib.)* Bye, Pirate Sam. / Yer a true pirate. / Thanks for everything.

PIRATE CAPTAIN FREDERICK. Thank you, Sam. I will cherish your gift and use it every day for as long as I live. One thing, though… *(Showing her the phone display.)* What does this say here?

SAM. Oh… That just says, "Battery two percent." Mmkay, byeee!

> *(SAM jumps off the plank. Time travel music takes SAM back to the present day.*)*
>
> *(Back in the present day, we see SAM on the deck of the Caribbean Queen. She comes to. Her GRANDPARENTS enter in a hurry. They wake SAM and embrace her.)*

GRANDMA. Oh, Sam. We found you.

GRANDPA. We were worried sick about you.

GRANDMA. When we couldn't find you after dinner we thought for sure you had fallen overboard.

> *(They all hug.)*

GRANDPA. Where were you?

SAM. I was…um…working.

GRANDPA. Working?

GRANDMA. You can at least tell us the truth, Sam.

SAM. I was, Grandma. There was…a lot of stuff that needed to be done around the ship and I took care of it for Captain Frederick. I mean, Captain Fred.

GRANDMA. Do you expect us to believe that?

SAM. Are you saying I'm not capable of working?

GRANDMA. It's just not like you, honey.

---

*This music is not included in the score. A license to produce *The Caribbean Queen* does not include a performance license for any third-party or copyrighted music. Licensees should create an original composition or use music in the public domain. For further information, please see Music Use Note on page 3.

GRANDPA. Really, Sam, we thought you were dead. The least you could have done was tell us you were hiding out somewhere using your phone.

SAM. I would have told you but I was really busy. Trust me.

GRANDMA. Here comes Captain Fred. I'm sure he can tell us all about the work you did for him.

GRANDPA. Yes, let's ask Captain Fred.

SAM. No, don't...

GRANDPA. I knew it.

GRANDMA. Captain Fred, our granddaughter has been missing all day and she wants us to believe she's been working on the ship.

SAM. Captain Fred, I –

CAPTAIN FRED. Hey there, Sailor Sam. Thanks for all your harrrd work. The ballroom looks fantastic. I haven't seen a floor that shiny since Riverdance was here.

GRANDPA. She mopped the floor?

CAPTAIN FRED. She sure did. And she coiled the sound cables and mended the tablecloths. And she did it all in time for the big karaoke party tonight. I trust you'll all be there.

GRANDPA. Sam did all that?

GRANDMA. Well, I'm very impressed, Sam. What's come over you?

SAM. Oh, just time travel...er, time to unravel a bit and think about what's really important. Now, how about we play some mini-golf before heading to the karaoke party.

GRANDMA. Oh, Sam, we'd love that.

GRANDPA. But first, let's take one of those selfie pictures you like so much...as a family.

SAM. Okay.

> (**SAM** *holds her hand out to take a selfie and again realizes she has no phone.*)

But we'll have to use your phone. Mine fell overboard.

GRANDMA. It what?

SAM. Long story.

GRANDMA. I guess we won't be taking any selfies!

SAM. We'll just have to remember this moment in our own minds.

>   *(A **YOUNG PASSENGER** wanders in looking at his/her cell phone.)*

CAPTAIN FRED. Well, it looks like everything is smooth sailing here. Now, if you folks'll excuse me, I've got some work to do.

Scene Six

(**CAPTAIN FRED** *approaches the* **YOUNG PASSENGER** *and speaks to him/her.*)

CAPTAIN FRED. Ahoy, sailor. You know, I really shouldn't tell you this because we encourage passengers not to use cell phones on the boat but heck, I guess I can let you in on a little secret... No, I shouldn't say it.

YOUNG PASSENGER. What? What were you going to say?

CAPTAIN FRED. Legend has it...there's Wi-Fi on this boat.

(*The* **YOUNG PASSENGER** *gasps.*)

[MUSIC NO. 06 "THE QUEEN OF THE OLD CARIBE (FINALE)"]

ALL. (*Except for* **YOUNG PASSENGER**.)
THROW OUT YOUR TROUBLES AND WORRIES
ABANDON YOUR CARES ON THE BREEZE
WE SAVED YOU A FIRST-CLASS SEAT
AND STOCKED UP YOUR FIRST-CLASS SUITE
WITH RED BULL AND CAMEMBERT CHEESE

CAPTAIN FRED. (*In a stage whisper.*) You get a better signal over by the Pirate Plank.

ALL.
WE'RE ON THE QUEEN OF THE OLD CARIBE
THE QUEEN OF THE OLD CARIBE
A VACAY SO SWEET AND SERENE
ABOARD THE OLD CARIBBEAN QUEEN!

End of Play

www.ingramcontent.com/pod-product-compliance
Lightning Source LLC
Chambersburg PA
CBHW051406290426
44108CB00015B/2179